HOW TO DEFEAT RELIGION
in 10 Easy Steps

T0096016

HOW TO DEFEAT RELIGION
in 10 Easy Steps

A Toolkit for Secular Activists

Ryan T. Cragun

PITCHSTONE PUBLISHING
Durham, North Carolina

Pitchstone Publishing
Durham, North Carolina 27705

To contact the publisher, please email info@pitchstonepublishing.com

10 9 8 7 6 5 4 3 2 1

Library of Congress Cataloging-in-Publication Data

Cragun, Ryan T.
  How to defeat religion in 10 easy steps : a toolkit for secular activists / Ryan T. Cragun.
     pages cm
  Includes bibliographical references.
  ISBN 978-1-63431-012-3 (pbk. : alk. paper)
  1. Religion—Controversial literature.   I. Title. II. Title: How to defeat religion in ten easy steps.
  BL2775.3.C73 2015
  200—dc23

                          2014042521

CONTENTS

INTRODUCTION

You know what the worst part about defeating religion is?

There are no losers.

I want to defeat religion.

What do I mean by "defeat"? I want to shrink religion—really fundamentalist religion—to the point that it is marginalized in U.S. society. I want to make religious fundamentalists the new flat-earthers—they should be so disliked that they run to the furthest reaches of America to hide. Religious fundamentalists should be so unpopular that politicians avoid them, rather than pander to them and turn to them for endorsements. Religion will be defeated when U.S. politicians refuse their endorsements and stop intoning the pandering platitude, "And may God bless the United States of America." Religion will be defeated when the media considers fundamentalists so extreme that they are cut off and provided no platform to voice their views and instead are targeted for ridicule. Religion will be defeated when people are too embarrassed to admit in public that they believe the earth is

6,000 years old. Religion will be defeated when no one tries to convert anyone else to his or her supernatural belief system. When the last strands of legitimacy religious fundamentalists have in society have been severed, religion will have been defeated. I don't imagine all religion will ever be gone, but I'll keep fighting religion until it has very little influence on politics, widespread social values, the media, science, sexuality, economics, charity, education, gender relations, and even federal holidays.

I'm actually not opposed to liberal religion, which tends to be accepting of science and modern human values. If people still find value in believing in things that cannot be proven to be true but also cannot be proven to be false, that's fine. Many people who try very hard to base their decisions on scientific findings, critical thinking, and logic still hold some beliefs that cannot be proven true or false (e.g., that someone loves them), and that will likely always be the case. But I am opposed to fundamentalist religion, religion that accepts scripture as literal, that rejects scientific findings that run counter to scripture, and that views the world as wholly black and white or good and evil. Fundamentalist religion is the type of religion I'd like to see defeated.

That religion could hypothetically be defeated without a calamitous collapse of society illustrates an important and very noteworthy characteristic of religion: religion is *not* necessary for society. Sociologists have been studying religion for over 150 years, and one of the earliest conceptualizations of religion was in terms of its functions for society. Religion can serve any or all of the following functions: to teach morality, to justify the right of the leaders of the society to rule, to justify oppression, and to reinforce group boundaries, among others. However, religion is not required for any of these functions. Morality can be based in secular philosophy. The right to lead can be based on an implicit or explicit social contract. Oppression has also been justified on racial, ethnic, gender, and sexual lines (though, of course, it shouldn't be justified or even exist). And there are plenty of groups to which one can belong that can reinforce group boundaries. Regardless of the functions of religion for society historically, there is no reason to believe religion is, today, necessary for society. And this isn't just an exercise in theory; there are a number of countries where religion is so substantially diminished in both existence and importance that it may as well be nonexistent (e.g., Estonia, Hungary, China, Vietnam, Finland, Sweden, Denmark, etc.). In short, from both theoretical and empirical perspectives, religion can be argued to be unnecessary for society.

Since religion is *not* necessary, you might then wonder, is religion desirable? I have mixed feelings on this one, since there are some reasons to think that religion is not a universally negative phenomenon. As a skeptical atheist and secular humanist, I directly benefit from religion in only one way: it is the primary focus of my research and therefore helps to justify the existence of my job. But if religion were defeated, I would have no problem changing the focus of my research to some other sociological phenomenon. Thus, for me, personally, religion is not desirable. Certainly others see religion as desirable and many people believe that religion is a net positive for the world. That is a complicated assertion that can, with great difficulty, be evaluated (though there is inherent subjectivity in doing so). I have attempted to do just that in a previous book, *What You Don't Know about Religion (but Should)*. In that book I found that, depending on the characteristics one desires in people and society, fundamentalist religion is absolutely not beneficial for humanity. However, I also concluded that certain forms of religion—liberal, nonliteralistic, modern, and egalitarian versions of religion—are not particularly harmful to society and may, in some ways, be beneficial. If someone wants to be religious today, liberal religion is the least harmful way to be so. This suggests, then, that religion is not necessary and fundamentalist religion is definitely not desirable. If one were to recognize that religion is not necessary and also believe that religion is not desirable, *what could one do to bring about its defeat?*

This question occurred to me on my way to a conference about—of all things—religion! In the fall of 2012, I was on a plane traveling to the annual meeting of the Society for the Scientific Study of Religion. I was reading the feature article in an issue of *Wired* magazine about "apocalypses" or threats that might dramatically change the entire world. The article, quite cogently, illustrated that these apocalypses were extremely unlikely. The "end of the world" rhetoric must have triggered something in my brain, which is often ruminating on religion. The thought that flashed into my mind was, "Could social science be used to defeat religion?" That was almost immediately followed by my own counter argument, "Well, yes, but why would you want to even consider that? You don't believe all religion is bad." But I couldn't get the thought out of my head. So, I reframed it to make it more palatable. "*Hypothetically*, if I wanted to defeat religion and had the power and influence to substantially change the necessary aspects of the social world, how would I go about it?" A variety of "steps" or changes to society came to mind. Those steps form the chapters of this book.

When I counted the steps and realized I had assembled ten, I couldn't help but think of another famous ten-step plan. I am referring, of course, to the ten-step plan of the revolutionary social theorist Karl Marx (with Friedrich Engels), who outlined ten steps to convert a capitalist economic system and government into a communist one. I have a great deal of respect for Marx as a social theorist, but my hypothetical steps aren't nearly as lofty in their aim as were his. He wanted to change the economy. My hypothetical steps would be geared toward defeating an already weakening element of society— religion.

As I thought about the ten steps, and a possible title for the book, I ultimately decided on *How to Defeat Religion in 10 Easy Steps*. The title is very much meant to be a juxtaposition that grabs people's attention. There are thousands of books that talk about how to lose weight or improve your sex life in a specified number of steps (3, 5, and 10 seem to be particularly popular). The idea, of course, is that it's simple—follow the steps and the end result will be what the author promises. Well, I'm not going to make any promises, but the social scientific evidence suggests that the ten steps I have outlined in this book could significantly undermine the strength and vitality of religion. So, the plan I outline should work, but I'm not including a money-back guarantee!

If you're reading this book, you are probably a secular activist, meaning you advocate for the separation of church and state, for government policies based on science and reason, and for the normalization of irreligion within society. You also likely self-identify as a humanist, atheist, agnostic, or freethinker, or some combination of these terms. If you don't, you're probably reading this trying to figure out what secular activists are planning (sneaky you!). Either way, I suspect most readers are invested either in trying to get people to leave religion or in trying to keep people from leaving religion. This may also mean you've been involved in debates or discussions in which one person has tried to change the religious/irreligious position of another. Debating or arguing over religion is not a very effective way to get someone to change his or her position. Why? Because, when people are attacked, their immediate response is to defend. There is a lot of research on how people do this when it comes to political views, but not as much with religious views. Debating religion with religious people has a tendency to reinforce existing beliefs: nonbelievers are typically confident they have shown the believer's beliefs are wrong while the believer either feels the opposite or draws upon his or her trump card: faith. The end result is that no one changes his or her views. Because debating religion is so ineffectual, at no point in this book do I recommend that secular activists debate the religious about religion. In fact, such debates probably do more to strengthen religion than weaken it as it makes it seem as though religious people have a credible defense for their beliefs. In a sense, it gives religious belief legitimacy, especially if the religious can get experts to debate them.

If we want to defeat religion, we have to do it *without* the religious realizing what we are doing. Religion is part of culture.

Because culture literally is how people view the world, trying to directly change someone's culture is nigh impossible. Think about it this way: How would you respond if someone came up to you and said, "Hi. I don't like how you view the world. Would you mind if I rewired your brain so you perceived the world the way I do?" If you're like me, you'd probably tell them to take a hike. If we want to succeed in defeating religion, we have to weaken religion around the religious.

Changing a culture slowly, concertedly, and with purpose can be done. My aim here is to illustrate how secular activists can subtly and effectively remove religion from a culture such that, when the religious realize what is happening, they will: (1) not be able to do anything about it and (2) already be so nonreligious that they won't want to fight what is happening.

I need to clarify an important issue before I move on to the ten steps: what I mean by religion. Religion is collective beliefs (and often rituals) relative to the supernatural. There are two key components in this definition. The first is that the beliefs and rituals have to be "collective." If just one person believes he is Jesus, he's insane. But if someone believes she is Jesus and has convinced 10,000 other people she is, then she has a religion (she may still be insane, but, for some reason, we don't typically consider socially constructed, *shared* "realities" insanity). So, religious beliefs or rituals have to be collective. The second key component of the definition is that these are beliefs or rituals that are relative to the supernatural. "Supernatural" refers to things that are outside the empirically verifiable natural world, like ghosts, demons, deities, and spirits. This definition includes the primary institutions and entities we think of as religions today, including Christianity,

Islam, Buddhism, Hinduism, and Judaism.

Finally, before I begin with the ten steps, I should note that, as is the case with Marx's ten steps toward communism, these ideas can be used in two ways. My ideal reader is the secular activist who would like to see the defeat of religion and is working toward that end, but who may need a game plan or toolkit to help make it happen. Of course, the religious, recognizing how religion would be weakened by instituting my recommended changes to society, could themselves take my recommendations and fight against religious decline by acting in an opposite manner. In fact, I believe—and point out in the relevant chapters—that the religious have already realized how some societal changes are already weakening religion and are currently attempting to counteract these changes.

Thus, I write this book with some trepidation. First, I *do* want to defeat religious fundamentalism, but I'm not opposed to liberal religion. So, I'm a little torn about the idea of defeating *all* religion. Second, in revealing to secular activists what they might want to do—providing them a playbook or toolkit—I'm also revealing "secrets" to the religious, who may fight or attempt to reverse the proposed steps. Perhaps my moral compass is misaligned, but I'm less bothered by either of these concerns than I am by the fact that no one else has suggested a similar social scientific plan of action that just might defeat religion.

STEP 1

Promote and Defend Secular Education

*Do you know what they call a Pentecostal
with a PhD?*

A miracle!

One of the primary functions of education in the United States
has been to educate and prepare the workforce for an economy
much different from the one that existed in the preindustrial
age. Prior to the rise of capitalism and subsequently the
industrial revolution, education was important for some, but
much less so for others. Changes in the economy have resulted
in the development of broad-level, nearly universal education
for young people. In 1800, just after the founding of the United
States, 74 percent of Americans worked in agriculture. By
1900, that number had dropped to 40 percent. And by 2000,
just 1.8 percent of Americans worked in agriculture.

Agricultural workers prior to the 1800s didn't need much if
any formal education to perform their jobs, and those working
in other areas often learned what they needed to know through

the master-apprentice system. What most young people needed to know to survive could be learned from their parents, from relatives, or from their masters. But as the economic system shifted and the industrial revolution took place, several things happened. First, capitalism resulted in a growing group of underemployed individuals or "laborers." Second, the skills required to work in various aspects of the new economy— particularly for those overseeing the laborers but also for the laborers themselves—shifted as well. Increasingly, being able to read, write, and do basic arithmetic became important.

The development of public education was rooted in multiple desires among its early advocates. One prominent desire was to educate the workforce for the capitalists, training future employees to read, write, and do basic math. Another desire was to inculcate morality. And widespread public education would also simply give kids something to do, as the idea of "adolescence" was just being created at this time. Of course, many children of laborers also worked, until government regulation forced them out of the workplace and into the schools. This meant that, despite being motivated by a desire to improve the life chances of the less affluent, widespread public education also reinforced the class structure, which is something it still does.

There is another function of education as well. Education can be—well, who are we kidding, *is*—used by governments to indoctrinate citizens into believing what the government wants them to believe. It was this function of religion that was used to attempt to assimilate Native Americans into the culture of those in power—white Anglo-Saxon Protestants (aka WASPs). It is this function of education that is used to teach children in the United States about all the benefits of capitalism and none of the potential problems, turning them into relatively mindless consumers. Karl Marx realized this function of education, which is why public education controlled by the government was one of his ten steps to communism.

Public education was mandatory in every U.S. state by 1918, though that mandate did not apply equally to every group; it was largely overlooked for minority groups like blacks and Native Americans. Despite the ever-growing provision of education due to the shifting economy, public education was not universally well-received or implemented. Many minority religions were suspect of public education precisely because of its utility in indoctrinating young people. The majority religious perspective in the United States until 2013 was Protestantism; today Protestants remain the largest religious group but make up less than 50 percent of the population. Early public schooling efforts included a fair amount of Protestant indoctrination in the schools at the primary and secondary (and even the tertiary levels). This Protestant indoctrination was problematic for minority religious groups, like Catholics, Jews, and Mormons, because it resulted in the indoctrination of their children into a different religious tradition. This indoctrination was opposed at various levels and in different ways. Many Catholics, not having much success opposing the Protestant establishment, developed their own system of parochial education to parallel public schools in order to prevent their children from receiving Protestant religious indoctrination. Eventually, the growing pluralism in the United States resulted in a number of court decisions that removed specific forms of school-sponsored religious indoctrination, like Bible readings and prayers led by school faculty and staff. These legal challenges were largely championed by religious minorities and nonreligious individuals, including, famously, *Engel v. Vitale* (1962) and *Abington School District v. Schempp* (1963), in which school-led prayer and Bible readings were declared unconstitutional. While voluntary *student-led* Bible studies and prayers are legally still allowed in schools, the curricula of public schools have largely shifted to a secular education devoid of religious indoctrination. Discussion of religion is, in many schools, largely confined to the humanities where it is discussed as myth (well, dead religions are discussed as myth; the rest are studied from a comparative perspective). The supposed removal of official-led religious indoctrination— it often continues informally—from public schools led to an outcry of its own, by the Protestant establishment, which began to claim that schools were, instead of teaching children religion, teaching them secular humanism (not really true, but wouldn't that be awesome?!?).

My point in describing this history is that minority religious (and nonreligious) groups in the United States did not want their children indoctrinated, and now that members of the largest religious group cannot mandate the religious indoctrination of both their kids and those of the minority at the hands of school officials, they are unhappy about it (see Katherine Stewart's book, *The Good News Club*, for how they have tried to reverse this situation). What both groups—(non) religious minorities and Protestants—implicitly recognize is the primary point I want to make in this chapter: schools are highly effective at persuading young minds. Because of our current system of education's efficiency at conveying information, it—flaws notwithstanding—is very effective at filling those minds with information.

But with what does it fill those young minds? It fills them with what government-run school boards dictate. The power of public education and government-mandated educational standards is that they determine what kids learn. While explicit, state-sanctioned religious indoctrination—that is, Protestantism—has largely been removed from the formal curriculum of most public schools, remnants of Protestantism remain. For instance, the myths told to school children about the origins of Thanksgiving are largely rooted in Protestant and white supremacist revisionism and do not reflect the latest historical understandings of the origins of that holiday. Even so, the Bible is no longer supposed to be read before the school day starts and teachers and staff aren't supposed to subject the students to prayers. The Protestant establishment realizes that its explicit ability to indoctrinate (and implicitly evangelize) is gone, which is why it has begun to fight public schooling. An increasing number of parents are opting to homeschool their children. For 36 percent of those parents, the explicitly stated reason for homeschooling their children is to provide religious instruction. Of course, many other religious parents send their kids to private, religious schools, and an increasing number of states provide vouchers so parents can do so.

Why are religious parents and religious clergy so concerned about secular education? Because they believe it will undermine religious beliefs. While that is less likely to happen before college, there is plenty of evidence that college, in particular, does substantially reduce religious orthodoxy and religious beliefs. The effects of education on religious affiliation and on religious participation are mixed, with some studies indicating no effect and others showing a slight increase in religious participation if people make it through college with their religious identity intact. But there is no real debate over the effect of secular education on religious beliefs. This is clearly illustrated in figure 1, which contrasts highest degree attained with view of the Bible—whether it is the literal word of God, the inspired word of God, or a book of fables.

As figure 1 shows, those with less than a high school education are the most likely to be biblical literalists. Additional education results in declines in biblical literalism. Among those with a graduate degree, 36 percent see the Bible as a book of fables and myths. In short, education—particularly higher education—undermines fundamentalist religious beliefs!

Responding to this pretty clear effect of education on religious belief, many religious groups have begun to develop

Figure 1. View of the Bible by educational attainment

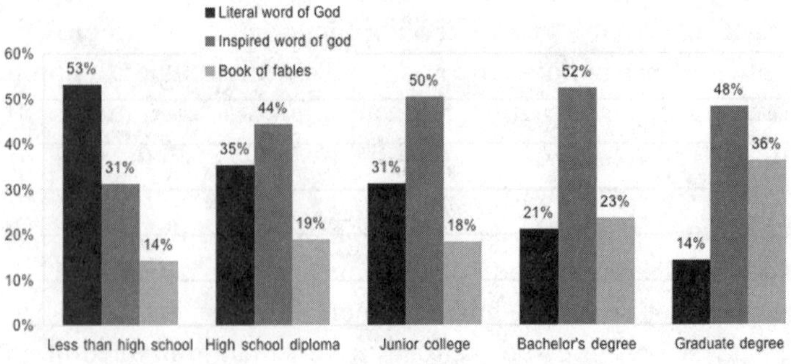

Legend:
- Literal word of God
- Inspired word of god
- Book of fables

Less than high school: 53%, 31%, 14%
High school diploma: 35%, 44%, 19%
Junior college: 31%, 50%, 18%
Bachelor's degree: 21%, 52%, 23%
Graduate degree: 14%, 48%, 36%

Source: GSS, 2012

their own systems of higher education as well, hoping it will counter the effects of secular education on religious orthodoxy. Catholics, Protestants, Mormons, Seventh-day Adventists, Hindus, Buddhists, and Jews all have institutions of higher education in the United States, and there are numerous Islamic universities outside the United States. The explicitly stated goal of many of these institutions is to provide a "secular" education in an environment that is safe for religious students (so, not a "secular" education).

I'm not the only one to argue that education is a threat to religion. Recent research suggests that the single best national-level indicator of religious decline around the world is level of educational attainment. While there are, as I will illustrate in the other chapters in this book, many aspects of modernization that contribute to the decline of religiosity, education appears to be a particularly important one. Why?

Education undermines religion in several ways. First, it can bring people of diverse backgrounds together (though this occurs primarily in college and less so in primary and secondary schools, which often reflect broader social segregation). Social scientists have long known that contact with people who are different from you reduces prejudice toward those people, and that includes contact with people who have a different religion. Thus, something as simple as getting to know people who don't share your religious worldview has the potential to call into question your worldview. College education can be very good at bringing diverse people together.

The second way education undermines religious belief is by discussing the existence of many worldviews. The result of such instruction can be and often is a realization that one's own view is subjective, leading to a recognition of the socially constructed nature of the social world. As people come to realize that society is socially constructed, it becomes much more difficult to accept the relatively common religious teaching that there are absolute truths and, particularly, that religions hold those truths. Religion comes to be recognized as just one more socially constructed institution. This, too, undermines religious belief.

Finally, education in modern countries often includes training in science, philosophy, and critical thinking. While science does not conflict with all religion, it does conflict with fundamentalist religion. That is, in fact, exactly why fundamentalist religion came into existence. Nonfundamentalist religions (i.e., moderate and liberal religions) are less likely to advocate views that conflict with science because they have adjusted to accommodate the findings of science. As scientific knowledge has advanced, the truth claims of these religions have receded. But the same cannot be said of fundamentalists. Religious fundamentalists continue to maintain absurd claims—like a worldwide flood or an earth that is 6,000 years old—despite the overwhelming scientific evidence illustrating those ideas are ridiculous. Students who attend public schools in the United States and pretty much every other modern country around the world will be exposed to scientific thinking, which can lead them to question their religious beliefs. Teaching science as method and not as "facts" would be even more effective at accomplishing this.

Of course, religious fundamentalists are already aware of how secular education is weakening religion. In the United

States, the religious are engaged in a protracted battle to undermine public education, attacking secular education from multiple angles. One well-known attack vector is the religious fundamentalist campaign to gain control of school boards, both at the local and state levels. When they are able to gain control over school boards, they gain control over curricula or what is taught in local schools. This can result in ridiculous efforts, like those in Texas to limit discussions about Thomas Jefferson's influence on early American ideas or revise understandings of slavery. Additional efforts include the systematic removal of racial, gender, and sexual minorities from U.S. history.

Another attack vector of religious fundamentalists is to lobby politicians to introduce voucher programs. While there are a number of conservative organizations that want to dismantle public schooling for a variety of reasons, a number of the partners for initiatives like National School Choice Week are faith-based. Voucher programs reduce the double-expenditure burden for private education. In states that have voucher programs, parents who send their kids to private schools receive a reduction in their taxes to offset the private school tuition they pay. Some of the most vocal lobbyists for these vouchers are advocates of religious education. The goal, of course, is to get their children out of public schools, where, despite their best efforts, the religious have been unable to explicitly reintegrate religion back into the curriculum. Many religious parents want their children educated in religious schools where they will be indoctrinated.

Another approach the religious have employed to undermine education in the United States is to increasingly lobby to cut funding for education and scientific research. In 2000, states paid, on average, 70 percent of the cost of education at four-year institutions of higher education, while student tuition covered about 30 percent. As of 2011, student tuition covered, on average, 52 percent of the cost of a student's education while states covered 48 percent. State funding for higher education has been declining in the United States, forcing universities and colleges to increase tuition costs to cover their expenses. Part of the higher costs is due to a recent flooding of administrators, turning universities into increasingly top-heavy institutions. But reduced government funding for higher education has made college more expensive for students. Likewise, government funding for scientific research is declining. In the 1960s, at the height of the Cold War, federal funding for scientific research in the United States topped 2 percent of GDP. It has been declining consistently since then and today is close to 0.75 percent of total GDP, and close to half of that is defense or military research. Higher education and scientific research have declined as priorities in the United States, precisely at a time when other countries are increasing their expenditures on scientific research and higher education.

To offset these losses, some academics are turning to other sources for funding, like conservative and religious foundations, which have a very specific agenda. A notorious instance of this can be seen in the case of sociology professor Mark Regnerus, who relied on a conservative think tank to fund his remarkably flawed study examining the influence of same-sex parenting on children. His study has been cited numerous times by the homophobes defending so-called traditional marriage, even though the American Sociological

Association—the professional organization for most U.S. sociologists—has repudiated the study. Another strategy religious fundamentalists and conservatives have employed is to fund "centers" that employ religious academics. For instance, riding the wave of popularity among religious conservatives for getting his flawed study published, Regnerus recently cofounded the Austin Institute for The Study of Family and Culture. Without knowing much about the staff of the institute, one might believe that the institute was simply an impartial think tank focusing on issues related to the family. Yet the institute is composed of conservative Christians who are pushing a very specific religious agenda and are lacking in the very areas of expertise they claim, like knowledge about sexual dynamics within families.

Religious fundamentalists in the United States would like nothing more than to gut secular education at every level—primary, secondary, and tertiary. To do this, they have tried to reintroduce religious indoctrination through initiatives like the intelligent-design wedge strategy, the Good News Club, and the Fellowship of Christian Athletes. They have also tried to take over the bodies that control curricula by stacking school boards with religious fundamentalists. And they have lobbied to reduce funding for secular education and research and instead have pushed for vouchers for religious education.

Education is a tool of those who are in power to indoctrinate citizens into the belief system those in power want the citizens to hold. Secular activists can use education precisely to this end. By gaining control over school curricula, activists can remove any element of religious indoctrination from schools and relegate instruction about religion to classes in the humanities and social studies, where religion can be studied as an object of inquiry, not as viable belief systems. Thus, one step in defeating religion is to gain control over the educational system and use it to promote and defend secular values (see chapter 10).

Now, I am not an expert on education. I'm not arguing that exerting substantial influence over the educational system would improve public education or solve any of the other problems education is facing in the United States. I'll leave those issues to the experts on education. My focus is on defeating religion. Step 1 in defeating religion then is ensuring that children are well educated *out*side a religious context and without religious indoctrination. Such education should also focus on critical thinking rather than rote memorization. What can secular activists do, especially in the United States?

Recommendations for Individual Secular Activists

- Run for your local school board.

- Volunteer in your local elementary, middle, and/or high schools. Volunteering has a dual purpose. Not only can you directly help children, but you can also watch for church-state violations, which you can report to national secular activist organizations.

- Write your political representatives regularly to advocate for more funding for higher education and science research.

Recommendations for Local Secular Activist Groups

- Send a representative from your group to attend local school board meetings. That representative can then report back to your group about what is happening at the local school board and, if there is reason for concern, the local group can take action to influence the school board's agenda.

- Even better than having a member of your group attend local school board meetings would be to organize a campaign to get a member of your group elected to the local school board. With the backing of a local secular activist group, that person would have lots of help in setting up and conducting his or her campaign, increasing the odds of success.

- Set up an essay competition for local middle-school and high-school students. The essay could be on a variety of topics, but here are two suggestions: Why is the separation between church and state important? What are the benefits of a secular democracy over a theocracy? Offer a $100 first prize and $50 second prize and make the contest a big deal in the school and local area. By getting students to write essays in favor of secular principles, the students will end up understanding the benefits of secularism in the process. In other words, the essay competition will actually function to create more advocates of secularism. If 100 students write essays and 50 become secular, that is well worth the investment.

Recommendations for National Secular Activist Organizations

- Lobby for national standards, like Common Core, in most areas of primary and secondary education. The effect of national standards in education is to remove control over curricula from the hands of local and state school boards. In particular, work with organizations like the American Association for the Advancement of Science to develop science curricula that is developed and approved by scientists. This will effectively tie the hands of local and state-level school boards in determining what their curricula can contain, undermining the efforts by the religious to gain control over school boards to manipulate curricula. While this recommendation seems to run counter to some of the recommendations for individuals and local secular activist groups, in practical terms, it's not counter to those recommendations. Although national standards are being developed, they have yet to be implemented, meaning local and state-level school boards remain important in determining curricula for schools. Until school boards have been largely neutered in their ability to determine curricula, secular activists should be represented on those boards. (Note: I don't think that Common Core—or any other universal curriculum—is perfect, but my inclination is to advocate for it so long as it is determined by a diverse panel of experts in their respective areas as opposed to religiously or politically motivated individuals on local school boards.)

- Given the size of national secular organizations, they are likely the only groups that would have the resources to develop specific course curricula that they could then offer to schools. Countering efforts by groups like the National Council on Bible Curriculum in Public Schools, national secular groups could hire *actual* Bible scholars to develop curricula and then fund an effort to have that curriculum on the Bible adopted in public schools to counter efforts by proreligious groups. Selling points for such a curriculum could be: (1) it is developed by leading experts on the Bible (e.g., Bart Ehrman, Hector Avalos, Reza Aslan, etc.); (2) it teaches the Bible based on a scholarly perspective, not a sectarian perspective; and (3) it is regularly updated to reflect the latest research on the Bible. Sure, most secular activists want religion out of public schools, but if it's going to be there, why not have religion taught the way we want it to be taught? And for cash-strapped national groups, the best part about this activity is that you may be able to make some money by selling the curriculum to schools.

• National activist organizations, in conjunction with local groups, could also spearhead a program to counter the Good News Club. One of two possible approaches could be taken toward this program. If the goal is to get the Good News Club out of public schools, the program should be named something outrageous, like "Christ and the Easter Bunny Club," "Why Jesus Wants You to Hate Your Mother Club," "Our Religion Is Right and Everyone Else Is Going to Hell Club," or the "Bribing Kids to Indoctrinate Them Club." The more outlandish the name, the better, as it will draw attention to this issue and the abuses of groups like the Good News Club and likely get them removed from the schools altogether. If the goal is to actually offer kids a secular alternative, however, the other approach would be to make the name more benign sounding and to create a serious alternative to the Good News Club. For example, the initiative could be called the Best News Club—or, the Better News Club, as a nontheistic after-school group in Rochester, New York has dubbed itself in direct response to the Good News Club. No matter the name, the goal would be to teach secular humanism and to counter religious indoctrination. Steal the techniques employed by the Good News Club and make the Best News Club more appealing. If you can't beat 'em, copy 'em!

STEP 2

Empower Gender, Sexual, and Racial Minorities

Did you hear the Catholic Church was going to start allowing women to be priests?

Yeah, neither did I.

Gender, sexual, and racial minorities could be some of the best allies of secularism. The reason is obvious—religion has a long history of oppressing and justifying the oppression of all of these groups. But secular activists have to address some serious problems within their ranks before this can occur. I'm going to discuss those problems and then suggest some things the secular movement can do to both recruit among and work with these groups, but before I do so, I need to explain what I mean by "minorities."

In sociology, somewhat misleadingly, we use the word "minority" to refer to any oppressed group. Thus, when I refer to "gender minorities," I'm including women who, in most countries around the world, including the United States, are actually the statistical majority (even though there are more men born than women, women outlive men). Also included as gender minorities would be anyone who is not cisgender (e.g., transgender and gender queer individuals); cisgender is an increasingly common term used to refer to individuals who identify their gender as male or female, in contrast to individuals who identify as transgender or gender queer. Sexual minorities would be anyone who is not heterosexual (e.g., lesbians, gays, bisexuals, etc.). Racial and ethnic minorities in the United States would be people who are not of a European and Caucasian or white background, such as African Americans, Hispanics, Native Americans, Asians, and people of mixed race. Thus, when I'm referring to gender, sexual, and racial minorities, I'm basically talking about everyone except white, heterosexual males, who, at present, make up the majority of secular activists. Several studies have found that white males make up between 55 and 65 percent of the membership of organized secular groups in the United States.

The fact that around 60 percent of secular activists in the United States are men, and most of them are white (I don't have good data on how many are heterosexual, but it's likely the vast majority), is likely a reflection of some of the problems that the secular movement has when it comes to recruiting gender, sexual, and racial minorities. Just as the preponderance of men in some natural science and engineering disciplines has restricted female recruitment due to higher rates of sexism and discrimination in those disciplines, it is possible that the high percentage of men (who are also predominantly white and likely heterosexual) in the secular movement is contributing to difficulties in recruiting gender, racial, and sexual minorities. While I don't have historical data on this issue, there have been some recent, notable accusations of sexual harassment and assault at secular conferences.

It seems as though things are beginning to change with the creation of new initiatives, including the annual Center for Inquiry–sponsored Women in Secularism conference and the national organization Secular Woman. But both of these initiatives are led by women who are trying to raise this as an issue within the broader secular movement and, while they have found some men who are strong allies, there are still many men, including some very prominent figures in the secular movement, who have been dismissive of the concerns of women. Likewise, I have read and overheard prejudicial comments toward sexual minorities among members of the secular movement. I have also spoken with African American atheists who are secular activists, and they have told me that they have faced discrimination as racial minorities.

I hate to think that the reason why some of these bigoted men (and, to a lesser degree, women) are so dismissive of the legitimate concerns of gender, sexual, and racial minorities is tied to their views of science, but I think it might be, and that is one of the other major problems the secular movement must address before it can become a safe place for gender, sexual, and racial minorities. I'm going to ask that you read this next section very carefully, as the argument I'm making is subtle and nuanced, but it is an important one. I'm going to discuss two ways to think about science (there are others). These two ways are not always easy to distinguish.

The first way to think about science is as a method of inquiry. From this perspective, you "do" science. Doing science means gathering data to test theories (deductive) or gathering data and developing theories to explain the data (inductive). Either way you "do" science, the goal is really to try to answer questions using the best-known method to date—the rigorous collection of empirical data. Recognizing that science is a method also admits that it is unlikely to be perfect. There are lots of ways that errors, flaws, and problems can enter into the "doing" of science, particularly since those people "doing" science are imperfect, often semi-rational individuals, many of whom have an agenda. While you are welcome to disagree with me on this, I think this perspective of science should be preferred.

The other way to think about science is to think about it as though it is a coherent, all-encompassing worldview. This perspective is often referred to as "scientism" and is basically a belief not only that science provides answers (in the methodological sense described above), but also that the only answers worth considering are those provided by science. Those who take this perspective will often assert things like, "Well, science says . . . " as though there is some monolithic, universal entity that has opinions (FYI, there isn't). In a sense, this is the "worship" of science.

This perspective on science is problematic. It's problematic because science does not offer a coherent worldview, for example, *the view of science*. This is particularly apparent once you take the first perspective described above into account, recognizing that science is, first and foremost, a method that is trying to help humans better understand things. Science, in and of itself, does not provide a coherent worldview, though it can help lay the foundations for a worldview. What's more, scientific findings regularly change. While religious people will often criticize "science" (really, scientific findings) for changing, one of the strengths of the scientific approach to answering questions is that it is typically self-correcting. When a scientist gets something wrong (because of flawed methods, because she was pursuing a particular agenda, etc.), future scientists can always revisit those findings by replicating the study. This doesn't necessarily mean it is easy to overturn scientific conventions, but it can be done, and often the greatest breakthroughs in our understanding of the natural world are based on the efforts of those who have questioned the scientific status quo.

My point in distinguishing between these two perspectives on science is to assert that one of the problems the secular community must address before it can become a safe place for gender, sexual, and racial minorities is a dogged insistence that science has all the answers or that science is always an accurate worldview (aka "scientism"). I know this is a sensitive subject. I identify as a scientist and try to do science. And I, too, often fall victim to thinking about science in the second sense because I am both a scientist and a lover of science. In fact, people visiting my home may have even observed my wife and I discussing issues only to have one or the other of us then ask, "Well, what does the peer-reviewed literature suggest?" We rely very heavily on science in making all sorts of decisions, about our health, how to raise our child, how to reduce our impact on the environment, etc. I'm a huge fan of science—as a method of inquiry that provides better (though not perfect) answers to questions we have about the natural world.

But science has also been used to justify some really horrible stuff. Slavery of Africans in the United States was justified using both religion and science, and later segregation was also justified using science. South African apartheid was developed by scientists. The eugenics movement, which resulted in the forced sterilization of millions of gender, sexual, and racial minorities (and many others), was justified using science. Reparative or conversion therapy for nonheterosexuals was originally developed by scientists when sexual orientation was considered by the leading scientific, psychological organizations as abnormal and in need of being "fixed." The continued effort to force parents to choose a "sex" for intersex individuals (and the resulting surgeries on nonconsenting children) is also largely justified using science. The widespread taboo surrounding masturbation—for men and women— was largely justified using nineteenth-century science, which was motivated by cultural and religious beliefs (e.g., "the sin of Onan"). As I'm writing this chapter, there are efforts being made by credentialed scientists (i.e., they have PhDs, tenure in scientific departments at prestigious universities, and have published their research in well-received, legitimate, scientific journals) to argue that same-sex marriage should not be legalized in the United States because their "science" calls into question the well-being of children raised in homes where the parents are of the same sex. I'm loath to call such bigots "scientists," but by all the standard measures, they are scientists.

These examples illustrate why I think it's important for secular activists to be very, very careful in how they think about science. Is science as a method superior to religion as a method for answering questions about the natural world? Of course! Absolutely! Yes! Yes! Yes!

But does science have all the answers? Is science perfect?

No and no! The secular community is right to embrace science. But secular activists should be wary to not embrace "scientism," which is basically the worship of science. Science is often wrong. Luckily, it can self-correct and often does. But scientific findings, when properly understood, are always tentative, pending further investigation. This is the attitude secular activists should hold toward science.

This is particularly the case when it comes to trying to recruit gender, sexual, and racial minorities to the movement. Why? Go back up a few paragraphs and reread some of the nasty things that have been justified using science. That's a short list, but think about how many of them targeted gender, sexual, and racial minorities. Science has often been used as a tool by those in power to justify their position of power and, for centuries, those in power in the United States have been white, heterosexual men. If you were a gender, sexual, or racial minority—a white lesbian woman, a biracial transgender individual, a gay black man, a bisexual Native American, a queer African American, etc.—how much trust would you put in a movement led by white, heterosexual men who treat science as though it is always right? If we're going to be honest, the answer would be, "Not very much!" In short, in order to recruit gender, sexual, and racial minorities, secular activists have to empower them, and doing so means being very careful in how we think about science. Science is great in lots of ways, particularly as a methodology for understanding the natural world. But secular activists should not fall prey to scientism.

Replacing religion with something that you treat the same way—that is, as "sacred" and "inviolate"—isn't really much of an improvement.

The first part of Step 2 to defeating religion is for secular activists to ditch the bigotry and scientism. But that's just the first part of recruiting gender, sexual, and racial minorities to the movement. The next part is helping to empower these individuals in and out of the movement and then recruiting them. I'm going to focus first on why the secular community needs women, then turn to why it needs other gender, sexual, and racial minorities.

There's a simple reason why the secular movement needs women: even in heterosexual relationships where men identify as feminists, when the couple has kids, women do the majority of child caretaking (obviously women do all the caretaking when the couple is lesbian, and, well, none when the couple is gay, but we'll turn to those couples in a minute). And when heterosexual couples split up, which happens with a large percentage of couples (~50 percent), women are more likely to get custody than are men. Guess what that means as far as child religiosity goes? Children are statistically more like their mothers than their fathers when it comes to religious belief and affiliation. If secular activists want more children to be raised secular, then secular activists needs to recruit more women. But, of course, there are plenty of other familial arrangements as well and, increasingly in the United States (and especially in other developed countries), children are being born to women who are not married. Most of those women are cohabiting, but the odds that a child spends some time in a single-parent-led home, most likely a female parent, are greater than 50 percent today. The secular community can't succeed if it doesn't recruit more women!

What about other gender and sexual minorities? Unless you've had your head stuck in a deep, dark place for the last forty years, you're probably aware that LGBTQ individuals have made tremendous strides toward equality (though we're obviously still far from equality in the United States). Increasingly, LGBTQ couples are also raising children, whether through birth or adoption. Thus, the same argument that I used above for why secular activists should want heterosexual women as part of the movement applies to why they should want LGBTQ individuals as part of the movement—LGBTQ individuals are raising kids. Of course, we want the LGBTQ individuals in the movement as well, but if you want kids raised secular, the best approach is to recruit their parents. Plus, LGBTQ individuals may actually outnumber religious nonbelievers in the United States. Yes, 20 percent of Americans are nonreligious, but not all of them are atheists, agnostics, freethinkers, or humanists—maybe half are. Which means LGBTQ individuals make up about the same percentage of Americans as do atheists, agnostics, freethinkers, and humanists, perhaps more.

And what about racial and ethnic minorities? The argument for this is just as simple as the others. Non-Hispanic whites in the United States are having fewer kids and fewer non-Hispanic whites are immigrating to the United States. According to the U.S. Census Bureau, non-Hispanic whites will become a minority in the United States in less than thirty years, 2043 to be exact. Just like most children are taken care of by women, and an increasing number are being raised by

LGBTQ individuals, more and more children in the United States are going to be raised by racial and ethnic minorities. If secular activists want to succeed, they need to broaden their membership to include racial and ethnic minorities.

Of course, I think secularism is a worldview that is more catholic than the Roman Catholic Church (note: "catholic" means universal). I think the secular worldview could work for everyone, but particularly for gender, sexual, and racial/ethnic minorities. But there's another reason why the secular movement should be recruiting among gender, sexual, and racial/ethnic minorities: many of these individuals have gained important experience working as part of a social movement for equal rights. Guess who could really use some help organizing a social movement for social equality in the United States? The secular movement!

Now I'd like to propose the biggest understatement of this book: recruiting gender, sexual, and racial minorities to the secular cause should be ridiculously easy. Why? Guess what has worked against gender, sexual, and racial equality every step of the way?

Religion!

So, this should be an easy sell. But, alas, the secular community hasn't always been an ally of gender, sexual, and racial minorities. Some prominent secular activists have actually been openly antagonistic toward these groups, albeit more so in the past than in recent years. Additionally, some religions in the United States, particularly liberal religions, have begun to change their views, doctrines, and policies to make them more appealing to all three of these groups. Religions have already realized the importance of recruiting this large segment of the population—the secular community needs to realize it, too!

What, specifically, can the secular movement do? Scholars have shown that, when single women are empowered through control over their fertility (see Step 4), control over their relationships (e.g., hookups, cohabitation, marriage, divorce, etc.), and control over their job prospects through equal educational opportunities and equal pay, they are more likely to reject religion. The secular movement needs to empower women in all of these ways.

But there is another issue when it comes to women and their involvement in religion that is rather intriguing. Religions have been the primary opponent to gender equality in the United States; literally, it was religion in the United States that killed the Equal Rights Amendment in the late 1970s and early 1980s. Scientists are not above criticism here as well. In part inspired by religious and cultural beliefs, scientists contributed to efforts to pathologize women's sexual, emotional, and biological experiences—for example, performing hysterectomies without women's consent or advocating for restrictions to birth control on the grounds that women were not capable of making their own decisions regarding their fertility. Thus, despite religion's opposition to gender equality, women tend to be more religious than men (this doesn't hold in all religions, but generally does in Judeo-Christian religions in the West). While there has been an increase in women looking outside of traditional religions for greater autonomy (e.g., New Age, Wicca, Paganism, lesbian book clubs) and feminist groups forming within religions, there is also a reason why some women are attracted to traditional religions. If women choose the Victorian ideal family arrangement—marriage, children, and household work—where are they most likely to find validation for this? In conservative and fundamentalist religions. In fact, in the United States, the ratio of women to men is most imbalanced in conservative and fundamentalist religions. Women who choose to stay home feel like their decision is better supported by religions than by secular values. Of course, this is not always or even typically a completely self-determined decision; often women have been taught that this is what they *should* want in religious and secular schools. What's the lesson for secular activists? If you want stay-at-home wives and mothers to become secular, you need to validate their life decisions too.

What about other gender and sexual minorities? As previously noted, religion has been and continues to be the primary basis for their oppression, marginalization, and discrimination. In a paper I recently coauthored, we argued that religion is the "last bastion" of prejudice, as religious people continue to believe that they can justify their hatred of and discrimination toward gender and sexual minorities with their religious beliefs. Because religion continues to be the primary opposition to equality for gender and sexual minorities, it should be remarkably easy to recruit such individuals into the secular movement, assuming, as I argued above, that we distance the secular movement from scientism and the now-obvious mistakes of past scientists. Yet, many LGBTQ individuals have turned to religion, in part because it has begun to adjust its doctrines and beliefs. Granted, the religions that cater to LGBTQ individuals, like the Metropolitan Community Church and the United Church of

Christ, are typically more egalitarian. Those religions are also not really the ones secular activists are or should be working to defeat. But it's pretty amazing to me that LGBTQ individuals want to have anything to do with religion given its despicable history on this front.

Why, then, do they continue to turn to religion? I discuss this more when examining Step 3, but part of the reason is that many LGBTQ individuals grew up with religion. When people feel threatened, as many LGBTQ people continue to feel in the United States, they tend to turn toward what they "know" or what is "traditional" for comfort. Thus, while many LGBTQ individuals do leave conservative and fundamentalist religions because they are so damaging to their identities, they still want to feel what they felt growing up, and they look toward liberal religions for that support, sense of community, and sense of familiarity. Of course, not all LGBTQ individuals turn toward religion; there are nonreligious support groups as well. Secular activists, if they want LGBTQ individuals to join the movement, need to think very carefully about the best way to reach out to these individuals and offer them support, empowerment, and safe communities without the religious baggage. Among the central tenets of humanism is tolerance for everyone, regardless of gender or sexual orientation. This is a huge selling point, and secular activists should be using it to attract gender and sexual minorities.

Finally, the secular movement has a lot to offer racial and ethnic minorities who, like gender and sexual minorities, have suffered extensively at the hands of religion. Religion was used both to justify the genocide of Native Americans and later to justify and facilitate their assimilation into their oppressors' culture. Religion was used to justify slavery for blacks. Religion has been used as the tool of empires for thousands of years to facilitate the conquest (see Step 8) of people around the world. In the United States, blacks used religion to help organize the Civil Rights Movement, though many prominent individuals in that movement were secular, as were many of the early feminists and suffragists in the movement for gender equality and many early LGBTQ activists. That is an important point, but so, too, is the fact that secular individuals only really tend to get involved in other causes when they believe it will hurt religions, which is problematic. The secular movement needs to be an active participant in working for the rights for all minorities, all the time.

In some ways, religion continues to facilitate some efforts among blacks to push toward racial equality. But here, too, the secular movement has a lot to offer. Why would blacks consider a book as deplorable as the Bible sacred? It was the primary justification of the slavery of many of their ancestors and continues to be used as the primary justification for white supremacy in the United States? Why would Hispanics continue to participate in the religion of the empire builders who often enslaved their ancestors and oppressed them, destroying their culture in the process? And why would Native Americans convert to or remain Christians once they realize that Christianity was used to justify the extermination of their ancestors and was the primary tool used to attempt to assimilate them into white, Anglo-Saxon Protestant culture? The secular movement needs to offer an alternative! Secular activists are failing so long as the secular movement remains underrepresented among the groups who stand to benefit the most from its perspective.

The second part of Step 2 in defeating religion is to empower gender, sexual, and racial/ethnic minorities. Here are some specific steps secular activists can take:

Recommendations for Individual Secular Activists

- First and foremost, secular activists need to be very careful in how they think about science. Science is the best epistemology currently available, but it isn't perfect. Science has contributed to the oppression of gender, sexual, and racial/ethnic minorities. When celebrating the scientific method and findings of science, secular activists should not engage in scientism.

- Second and incredibly important, don't be chauvinists, color-blind racists, or homo/bi/transphobes! When secular minorities tell you that they are facing prejudice and discrimination in the secular movement, don't dismiss them. Listen to them. And fix the problem. If the secular movement wants to succeed, it needs to recruit minorities. That is not going to happen if white, heterosexual males are harassing, demeaning, or marginalizing minorities. Examine your own circle of friends. How racially and sexually diverse is it? Why? If most of your friends are just like you, maybe you need to broaden your circle of friends.

Recommendations for Local Secular Activist Groups

- In order to undermine religion's stranglehold on "family values," create interest groups in your local organization that are geared specifically toward stay-at-home mothers or parents with young kids. I receive advertisements from a church near my house every few months that advertises things like free family photos, family picnics, Easter egg hunts, game nights for kids, etc. Religions know who their target audience is. Copy them. But do it better. Target LGBTQ parents (single, cohabiting, married, or polyamorous) along with heterosexual parents and make the activities for the kids fun and minority inclusive.

- Look at the members of your group. If almost all of them are male, white, educated, and/or heterosexual, you've got a problem. You need to reach out to gender, sexual, and racial/ethnic minorities. Invite some to come present to your group. Advertise your group activities in locations where these minority groups are likely to see the advertisements. Invite gender, sexual, and racial minorities to present "our story" (in contrast to *his*tory) presentations to correct scientific discrimination in textbooks. Diversify.

- Consider offering "commitment ceremonies" for cohabiting couples to help validate their relationships without supporting marriage. Increasing numbers of Americans are opting not to marry, which alienates them from religions. Welcome them into your secular group by supporting their decision to cohabit and have sex (and children) outside of marriage.

- Be open to conceptions of family and experience that go beyond those often extolled by religions. Create interest groups in your organizations that are geared toward promoting and affirming the diversity of lifestyles, arrangements, and experiences of a wide array of people.

Promote and host activities for childfree people.

Recommendations for National Secular Activist Organizations

- Consider advertising in magazines, media, and other locations that are specifically geared toward minority gender, sexual, and racial/ethnic groups. Here are some suggestions for ads:

  » "We're not fighting against your rights, we're fighting for them."

  » "Religion: The Last Bastion of Sexual/Gender Prejudice"

  » "You know what religion is good for? Justifying prejudice!"

  » "Well-behaved women seldom make herstory."

  » Or just quote scriptures like these and add below them "Disagree? So do we!":

    · "If a man has sexual relations with a man as one does with a woman, both of them have done what is detestable. They are to be put to death; their blood will be on their own heads." Leviticus 20:13

    · "All who are under the yoke of slavery should consider their masters worthy of full respect, so that God's name and our teaching may not be slandered." 1 Timothy 6:1

- Form coalitions that support minority rights, working with groups like NOW, the Human Rights Campaign, the NAACP, Planned Parenthood, etc.

- Show that you're serious about diversity by hiring and promoting minorities in your organizations. Of the four largest secular groups in the United States (i.e., American Humanist Association, American Atheists, Freedom From Religion Foundation, and Council for Secular Humanism), three are headed by men and the fourth is headed by a husband-wife duo. (Many members of the boards of these organizations are female and do reflect diversity, but female leadership would send an important message.) All of these leaders are white (though one identifies as Native American) and heterosexual. The "four horsemen" of New Atheism—Richard Dawkins, Christopher Hitchens, Sam Harris, and Daniel Dennett—are also all white, heterosexual males. That looks an awful lot like a patriarchal heteronormative movement. It would be easier to recruit more minorities into the movement if the leadership was more diverse. Of course, there have been some recent efforts on this front, with the creation of Secular Woman, Black Nonbelievers, Hispanic American Freethinkers, and other groups targeting these demographics, all of which suggests that these groups are interested in joining the movement. That is progress, but more can be done.

STEP 3

Provide "This Life" Security

Have a "fish fry" at church, and people will eat for a day—and go to church.

Have universal healthcare, retirement benefits, reproductive justice, family leave, and disability benefits, and people will always have food—and stop going to church.

Disease.
Poverty.
Homelessness.
Famine.
Death.

If you're like most people, when you read or hear these words, your response, try as you might, is an emotional one: fear! That's not all that surprising. But what is surprising, is the various ways in which most people respond to fear. While researchers are somewhat conflicted as to why exactly people look for security and comfort when afraid, this basic response is universal: fear leads people to want security and comfort, wherever and however they can find it.

Now let's consider religion in a hypothetical scenario. Let's presume that Bob is a poor, subsistence farmer in rural America in the late 1700s. Weather patterns—which are beyond his control—have not aligned with typical patterns and, as a result, his crops are dying. Without his crops, Bob is going to suffer and the odds of his death increase pretty substantially. Bob is more likely to suffer: disease, poverty, homelessness, famine, and death. What does Bob do?

Of course, he could turn to others for help. He could try planting something else, assuming he has the resources to do so. He could turn to hunting and gathering, though, in all likelihood, he's also doing that to feed himself and his family, since he's already a poor subsistence farmer. But, more than likely, he will turn to a source that will give him comfort and security: religion. Bob may not be able to control the weather, but he believes there is something that can, his God or gods. When humans can't do anything else to alleviate their fear, it is pretty common for them to turn to supernatural forces for support, comfort, and security.

Now, I could assert things here like, "Nothing fails like prayer" or "It's just pretend." I could do that. But that misses the entire purpose of why Bob is praying: he's scared! Bob doesn't need mockery. Bob needs security. He needs comfort. He needs to reduce his anxiety.

Now let's consider a different hypothetical scenario. Anders is a self-employed farmer in Denmark in 2014. Because of the tax and welfare system of the Danish government, what happens to Anders if he loses his crop? Is he more likely to get sick? No. He has guaranteed healthcare through the government. Is he more likely to become poor? No. Danes have unemployment insurance and a substantial subsidy system. Is he likely to lose his home? No. His unemployment payments will allow him to keep making mortgage payments. Is he likely to starve? No. His unemployment payments will make sure he can eat. Is he likely to die? No, because of the Danish social safety net. How much anxiety does Anders experience as a result of the noncooperative weather? I'm sure he'll experience some. And I'm sure he'll be bothered by the poor weather because he probably takes some pride in his work and is pleased when he can successfully contribute to his country's economy and can help feed other people. But it is not going to induce fears of disease, poverty, homelessness, famine, or death, because there is a substantial public safety net in place for just these types of situations. Anders may worry, but he's not going to turn to a God or gods for help. He'll turn to the government.

In countries where the government provides extensive social welfare—health benefits, unemployment benefits, disability benefits, and retirement benefits—people tend to be less religious. Where governments don't offer such benefits, people tend to be more religious. Religion, for many people, serves a compensatory function. When life is challenging, when resources are limited, when your future is bleak, when you are deep in the throes of fear, the promises religions make are very attractive because they are comforting.

Many religions promise immortality, though in differing forms. For Jews, Christians, and Muslims, immortality is retaining your identity and living in the presence of a God. For Buddhists and Hindus, it's losing your identity and attaining nirvana—a oneness with the essence that makes up everything. Other religions offer variations on one of these two themes. But the important point is that religions promise something other than annihilation at death. Regardless of the form, you're going to continue to live. Now, isn't that comforting?

Of course, for many secular activists who have thought this through, it may not be all that comforting. Mark Twain's book mocking the Christian conception of heaven, *Captain Stormfield's Visit to Heaven*, provides one reason—heaven would be ridiculously boring! Plus, given the characteristics of the Jewish/Christian/Muslim God, who would actually want to hang out with that jerk—and for eternity!?! Okay, but logical thinking aside, the idea that you don't actually die when you die kind of, sort of, seems comforting.

But religions offer other compensatory functions as well. Many religions offer rationales for suffering. Yes, you may have lost your arms and legs in a bizarre dishwasher accident, but that's part of God's plan to make you more humble. Sure, your lesbian partner and adopted children were killed in a natural disaster, but that's part of God's plan to help turn you straight. And your boss may be a real jerk who sexually harasses you, but this is to help you overcome suffering so you can be reincarnated into a higher form in the next life. Many religions offer justifications for inequality, which will also be addressed in the afterlife. If you're poor or rich in this life, for most religions that doesn't have any real influence on whether or not you are rewarded in the afterlife (though it may be a reflection of what you did in a past life). Thus, religions provide a salve for suffering in this life and a promise of a better future in the next. Religion, then, can and does provide security for those who cannot find security elsewhere: life may suck and your body is going to die, but it is only temporary and it is part of a higher plan.

People buy into this . . . until they don't have to anymore. People living in countries that become more affluent begin to swap out supernatural security for natural security. If a government promises its citizens food to eat, a place to live, healthcare, and a minimum standard of living throughout their lives, people turn away from religion for their security needs. Others have illustrated this statistically, but I think it's useful to do so in a very simplified way. Let's move our hypothetical Bob into the twenty-first century but keep him in the United States. And let's move Anders from Denmark to Sweden, since I have data on Sweden but not on Denmark and they have very similar social safety nets. Now, let's say that Bob and Anders are the same sex, the same age, have the same level of education, and the same income, which is something we can do statistically. The only difference between the two is that Bob lives in the United States and Anders lives in Sweden. How important is living in Sweden on Anders' likelihood of believing in God? Just because Anders lives in Sweden, he is 22 times less likely to believe in God—inversely, Bob is 22 times more likely to believe in God!

To put this into perspective, looking just at the United States and Sweden, females are two times more likely to believe in God than are males, and every year of age makes someone 1.02 times more likely to believe in God, which isn't all that much from year to year, but adds up over 40 years.

Twenty-two times less likely to believe in God is astounding! That's about the difference between Mount Everest, at 29,029 feet, the highest point on earth, and the highest hill in Ohio, Campbell Hill, which is 1,539 feet.

What accounts for the difference in likelihood of believing in God between Bob and Anders? Certainly there are other things, like the general differences in culture in the respective countries. But the primary difference reflected in that number is that Sweden offers an extensive social safety net and the United States doesn't. If Bob were working for a large corporation instead of farming and lost his job today in the United States, what else would he lose? Well, he'd get temporary unemployment for as much as a year, then he would receive no more help from the government. He'd lose his healthcare from his employer, but he'd eventually be covered by the federal government once his income dropped below poverty levels thanks to the Affordable Care Act (aka Obamacare). He'd likely lose his house. He may eventually qualify for food stamps, but even those are being cut back. Bob faces poverty, increased likelihood of disease, increased likelihood of homelessness, increased likelihood of hunger, and increased likelihood of death, just because he lost his job. That would make me afraid, doubly so, since I have a young son who relies on his mother and me for his food, shelter, and security.

So, what do we do? Well, libertarians and conservatives aren't going to like this, but the answer is simple: provide an extensive social safety net. If your primary goal is to defeat religion, then one of the most effective ways to do that is to provide natural, mortal security so people don't have to turn to supernatural sources for faux security. The United States should have: universal healthcare for everyone, indefinite unemployment benefits, excellent family and medical leave benefits, retirement benefits, reproductive health benefits, and disability benefits.

Does this mean we all have to be socialists?

No. Of course not.

I hate it when people think that capitalism and socialism are mutually exclusive options. Guess what the military, public libraries, the police, the fire department, the post office, public schools, our transportation system, and most of higher education have in common? They are all socialist-like. They are paid for with tax dollars and are run by the government. They are not run by private corporations. And before you say, "Oh, but they should be. I hear the post office is losing money every year," let me ask you something: which corporation do you want to run the police department in your area?

"Hello, this is 911, what's your emergency?"

"Someone is trying to break into my house."

"What's your credit card number, ma'am? As soon as your card clears, I'll send someone to help."

You see, capitalism and socialism are not either/or options. The United States already has aspects of socialism, and some of them are things you really, really want to be socialistic, like the military, the police, and the fire department. What it does mean is that we should move closer toward socialism, while retaining some of the positive aspects of capitalism, like competition between businesses for nonessential items, such as cars and cellphones. In fact, from the 1940s to the 1970s, the United States was more socialistic than it is today; economic inequality was lower than it is today, and that socialist-capitalist balance is basically what most other developed countries have today. Regulated capitalism is the same thing as regulated socialism; it's a continuum, not a dichotomy.

An interesting thought occurs to me here. The Republican Party has, over the last forty or so years, allied itself closely with the Religious Right. While most political scientists will argue that the reason that religious conservatives have allied with the Republican Party is because of its positions on social issues, where their views generally align, sometimes I wonder if there isn't a bigger vision here, at least for the upper echelon of religious leaders in the United States. It's pretty clear that, according to the media, most of the opposition to a broader social safety net comes from wealthy individuals who don't want to pay more in taxes (the highest tax rates in Denmark are over 60 percent, which is still lower than the historical highs in the United States, which were over 95 percent). But there is also reason to believe that, at least at some point, some conservatives were aware of what I explained in this chapter: social safety nets reduce demand for religion. The neoliberalism that came to power in the 1980s was, at least in part, driven by a conservative economic agenda that hoped to divide progressive movements (e.g., abortion rights, women's rights, sexual minorities' rights, workers' rights, etc.), so everyone from the middle class on down would overlook the concentration of wealth and power among an economic elite. Part of Ronald Reagan's agenda during this time was an attempt to undermine progressive politics, and he acknowledged that the end result would be economic desperation for most people, driving them back into the arms of the churches. To what extent the leadership of the Religious Right and conservative politicians are still thinking about this, I can't say. But sometimes I wonder.

There's another reason why I wonder. Upper-echelon religious leaders are also often very affluent. For those individuals, they are likely doubly motivated: they oppose higher taxes on the rich because they are the rich, but could they also be knowledgeable enough about the relationship between social safety nets and levels of religiosity that they may specifically oppose widespread social welfare to ensure they have a reliable source of income (i.e., religious people)? It's self-serving and immoral, but not beneath individuals selling empty promises in order to buy luxury homes and afford private jets.

In addition to general welfare programs that provide this-world security, there are other programs that I think can and should be fully supported by secular activists if they want to see the demise of religion. I regularly visit religions as a social scientist, observing what is happening. In most of the congregations I have visited, I have seen and often interacted with individuals who are "socially awkward." These individuals, who claim to believe and are often very actively involved in the church, find an accepting community in the congregation. Their dedication to the congregation gains them admittance and acceptance, which, in many cases, is really what they are trying to gain. Whatever the reason for their social awkwardness—personality disorder, psychological condition, kinks, or quirks, etc.—the religion accepts them.

I have also visited many secular groups. Some of these groups have had similarly socially awkward individuals who are regular participants. Their participation is often no less driven by social acceptance than is the case of many who join religions. The lesson here should be clear: social groups that are organized around a shared belief system provide an accepting community for individuals who struggle with social acceptance. Such individuals still need a home if/when religion is defeated. Those freethought and nonreligious groups that welcome such individuals into their groups are helping to facilitate the transition to a nonreligious society. But, more widespread efforts need to be made in this regard. These groups should focus more on shared beliefs regarding economic equality, diversity, and tolerance. Whether government programs are developed or nonreligious groups engage in concerted outreach to invite such individuals into their folds, this is one function of religion—providing a community for those who can't find it elsewhere—that should also be filled. Thus, secular activists should keep this population in mind when working to defeat religion.

What, then, can you do to provide this-life security? Here are some suggestions.

Recommendations for Individual Secular Activists

- Send your religious nieces and nephews to Sweden or Denmark for a study-abroad program.

- Pay your taxes and don't complain about government programs specifically geared toward providing a social safety net.

- Vote for politicians who advocate a broad social safety net.

Recommendations for Local Secular Activist Groups

- Volunteer, collectively, for campaigns for candidates who want broad social safety nets. Build secular groups around a shared belief in equality and justice. Humanism— the primary ethical perspective of most religious nonbelievers—values more than just science; make that manifest in your groups by advocating for reduced economic inequality.

- Welcome socially awkward or otherwise socially rejected people into your groups. They, too, want security and comfort, as well as general acceptance. If you reject them, chances are they will find acceptance in a religious congregation.

- Set up a local nonprofit organization to help people transitioning out of prison. These people are particularly vulnerable when it comes to social safety nets and social rejection. If you can help them reintegrate into society, you not only will be helping the vulnerable, but you also could get some money from the government to facilitate the program. Many religious groups do this, and they use it as an opportunity to proselytize. So can you.

Recommendations for National Secular Activist Organizations

- Make a broad social safety net part of your general platform. Some national level secular groups tend to be more libertarian in this regard. I understand the appeal of libertarianism—when you're at the top of the social ladder. But libertarian ideals are counterproductive if you really want to defeat religion, as the people at the bottom of the social ladder are going to turn somewhere for their security, and if that somewhere isn't the government, it's going to be religion.

- Include articles about the religion-reducing benefits of broad social safety nets in your magazines and newsletters to spread the word.

- Lobby for broader social safety nets with politicians at the local, state, and national levels.

STEP 4

Encourage Sexual Liberation for Everyone

The best sex advice . . . doesn't come from the Pope.

Imagine for a moment that you're in your mid-twenties and single. Now pretend that your parents raised you as a member of an organization to which they also belong that they think is really important. Let's call that organization "People Rejecting Ungodly Desires Early," or PRUDE. One of the values of PRUDE, detailed explicitly in its statement of core values, is that members of the organization can only have sex within marriage. Any form of extramarital sex—premarital sex, or sex with someone other than one's legal spouse—is strictly prohibited by the organization. Anyone caught violating this value will be punished by the organization through public shaming and, potentially, expulsion. To continue our hypothetical exercise, let's now say that you meet someone you find attractive, you begin to see the person regularly, and you eventually become very close. Then, of course, it happens. As you're snuggling on a couch one night after a very enjoyable date, one thing leads to another and . . . you have awesome sex!

Uh-oh. Now you have a problem. What about your involvement with PRUDE? You violated one of the core values. As a result, you experience inner turmoil (i.e., "cognitive dissonance"). What should you do? You could stop having amazing sex with this really cool person in order to return to the good graces of this organization to which you have little loyalty but to which your parents place great importance. Or, you could stop going to PRUDE meetings and stop identifying as a PRUDE. Either option will reduce the inner turmoil you feel as your personal values will then align with your actions. Your sexual partner is not a PRUDE and doesn't really understand why you are so conflicted over sex. What's more, almost everyone you know is also having sex—whether married, cohabiting, or single. So, what do you do?

My hypothetical example isn't all that hypothetical. It is basically what is happening with young people across the United States and around the world every day. Close to 95 percent of young people in the United States have sex before marriage. More and more young people are cohabiting before marriage, and an increasing percentage of the population thinks cohabiting before marriage is a good idea. What does this have to do with defeating religion? When people engage in behaviors that run counter to the values of their religion, they feel conflicted. One very easy solution to resolving this conflict is to leave the religion or, at the very least, stop attending religious services. That appears to be happening, and the data back that up. People who cohabit before marriage are less religious than those who do not cohabit before marriage.

Figure 2. Percentage of cohabiters and noncohabiters who are religious and nonreligious

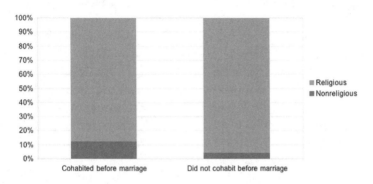

Source: GSS, 1988 & 1994

Figure 2 shows the percentage of people who cohabited before marriage (first column) and those who did not (second column) contrasted with whether or not they report a religious affiliation. Of those who cohabited before marriage, 12.3 percent are nonreligious. Of those who did not cohabit before marriage, just 4.3 percent are nonreligious.

Cohabiting before marriage also reduces how often people attend religious services. The same dataset, the General Social Survey, finds that, of those who cohabited before marriage, 21 percent never attend religious services, 43 percent infrequently attend them, and 36 percent attend them fairly regularly. Among those who did not cohabit before marriage, just 11 percent never attend religious services, while 26 percent attend them infrequently and 63 percent attend them regularly.

I hate to get all technical regarding this data, but it's worth it for just a second. First, because of the nature of the questions asked, a causal relationship can be suggested here, though with some caution. Because the people who answered the question about having cohabited before marriage are or were married at the time they participated in the survey, their cohabitation must necessarily have taken place in the past. And since they were asked about their religious affiliation and religious service attendance in the present, then what we can deduce is that their cohabitating came before their current religious affiliation and attendance. So, it meets one key criteria of causality—preceding the second event in time. Second, it is true that those who are raised nonreligious are more likely to cohabit before marriage, which accounts for some of the difference in cohabiters being less religious. But in more complicated regression analyses, whether or not someone cohabited before marriage is a stronger predictor of religious attendance and religious affiliation than are either being male or having no religious affiliation at age sixteen. Cohabiting significantly and substantially reduces how involved with religion people are. In simpler terms, cohabiting helps to defeat religion.

Okay, but why? Most religions have tried to regulate sexuality. That is, simultaneously, very smart and also very stupid. When religions can, successfully, regulate sexuality, they control perhaps the most powerful aspect of many people's lives. There is no better way to illustrate absolute domination over someone else than to control his or her sexuality. My favorite example of this was Wayne Bent, a cult leader in New Mexico in the 1990s and early 2000s, who claimed that God wanted him to sleep with his daughter-in-law. His son conceded. This is all documented in a National

Geographic Channel special on the cult. The look on his son's face in the interview when he was asked about letting his wife sleep with his father was one of the most stunning examples of absolute submission I have ever seen. Wayne Bent controlled every aspect of his son, from his mind to his penis. When religions are able to successfully regulate the sexuality of their members, they have near absolute power and control over their members' lives.

But, religions trying to regulate sexuality is also incredibly stupid. As the hypothetical example about PRUDE illustrated, people are having sex, married or not. And they are going to continue having sex, whether religious or not. Humans are perhaps the most sexual animals in existence. We spend more time thinking about, talking about, trying to get, and having sex than most other mammals. We are extremely intimate beings who exhibit a wide variety of sexual diversity.

Sexual mores regularly shift in the United States. For example, Americans had more sex prior to the Victorian era than they did during that era in the late 1800s and early 1900s. They were also more knowledgeable about sex until religion and science were both used to justify sexual oppression. Shifting social arrangements (like larger households with separate rooms for parents and kids) also resulted in less knowledge about sex. Why would large homes do this? When a family all lives in a one-room home, where do the adults have sex? Yep, right next to the kids!

By the 1950s, Americans had actually reached an apex of both sexual repression and sexual ignorance. But that is changing. Just 12 percent of people born before 1900 said premarital sex was not wrong at all in the General Social

Survey, but 57 percent of those born between 1980 and 1994 said premarital sex was not wrong at all. As sexual mores have shifted toward more open sexual expression in the last fifty years, religion has lost control over people's sexuality, even though many religions continue to try to assert such control, as seen in recent efforts to encourage marriage—and abstinence before marriage. As a result, religions that continue to oppose extramarital sex are setting themselves up to lose members who have sex and then decide that feeling guilty over it just isn't worth it.

Step 4 in defeating religion in the United States is to do everything possible to sexually liberate people. Here are some things you can do:

Recommendations for Individual Secular Activists

- Write to your political representatives to defund abstinence-only education and to fund real sex education. Lobby your school board to do the same.

- If abstinence-only sex education is being taught in your local school district, protest! And if you're a member of a local secular activist group, offer a free alternative sex education course for students and their parents (see suggestions for local secular activist groups).

- If you have kids, talk to them about sex. But, more than that, let them have sex in your house. Many American parents are ridiculous on this point, unlike their European counterparts. American parents are less likely to talk to their kids about sex, and they have unrealistic expectations that their teenage children: (1) are not having sex (they are); won't have sex until marriage (they will); and are open about having sex (they're not because of parents' expectations). In Europe, parents not only expect that their teenage children will likely have sex, but they also talk to them openly about it and provide a safe, supportive environment for them to have sex—their home! Think about it this way: if your teenager is having sex in your house, not only will you know he or she is having sex, but you also can make sure that he or she is using birth control and condoms. You can make sure that the sex is as safe as possible. Don't be a member of PRUDE!

Recommendations for Local Secular Activist Groups

- Reach out to cohabiting couples. Start an advertising campaign specifically for cohabiting couples. Let them know that you support people having sex, married or not. You could advertise in bridal magazines, on billboards, or even on buses. Some possible advertising lines you could use:

  » "Tired of feeling judged? So were we."

  » "Religion: The Last Bastion of Sexual/Gender Prejudice"

  » "God's not watching. %uck away!"

  » "Cohabitation: Humanist Approved!"

- If you're feeling particularly frisky, target some advertising toward childfree, swinger, nudist, polyamorous, and alternative sexuality groups. We don't have much data on the religiosity of members of those groups, but it's fairly likely that any members who are religious feel some conflict over participating in them. Since these groups (in contrast to our dominant social ideals and the goals of religious groups) emphasize sexual pleasure instead of reproduction, they are potential allies in our efforts to wrestle sexual discourse away from religious leaders. Give them an alternative. Some possible advertising lines you could use:

» "Like doing it in groups? So do we!"

» "You reject clothes; we reject faith. Let's talk!"

» "The Bible says, 'Multiply, and replenish the earth'; We think it's 'plenished' enough!"

» "Sex! It's about the pleasure!"

» "'But [we] tell you that anyone who looks at [someone else] lustfully . . .' is human!"

- If any members of your local group have extensive training in human sexuality, your group could volunteer to teach sex education classes in local schools or for local adults. The lack of knowledge most adults have about sex is pretty stunning. You could make this a regular event—hold a completely open sex education class once a year with an expert on sex and invite people to ask whatever they want. You can probably find an expert at your local university or contact me for suggestions.

Recommendations for National Secular Activist Organizations

- You could scale up one of the advertising campaigns I suggested for local secular activist groups. One good angle to take would be to emphasize the inherent inequality resulting from marriage, since married couples receive numerous benefits that nonmarried individuals do not receive.

- Make sex education a key platform issue for your organization. Whenever possible, lobby for good sex education. Run special issues of your magazines and newsletters that focus on sex education. You could even discuss topics like parents letting their kids have sex in their homes, as I outlined for individual secular activists.

- Various religious groups around the United States are making money teaching abstinence-only sex education courses in schools or developing curricula that they then sell to the schools. They also get a lot of that money from the federal government. Develop an "Abstinence-Only (Until You're Ready to Have Sex)" curriculum and then apply for money from the federal government to teach your program or spread your curriculum to local schools. If politicians won't defund abstinence-only sex education, then I don't see why secular activists can't take the money under the guise that we are teaching abstinence-only sex education and then actually teaching students real sex education. If politicians aren't basing their funding decisions off of the science that shows abstinence-only sex education doesn't work, then why should national secular activist groups have to base the title of their sex education curriculum on the contents?

STEP 5

Stop Subsidizing Religion and Deregulate It

A pastor, a CEO, and a politician all died in a plane crash. As they approached the gates of heaven, Saint Peter stopped them to determine if they were worthy to get in. He first asked the pastor a question, "What did you do to better humanity?"

The pastor responded, "I lied to people to give them hope."

Saint Peter nodded, then turned to the CEO and asked him the same question, "What did you do to better humanity?"

The CEO said, "I hired people to make myself rich."

Saint Peter nodded again then turned to the politician and asked him the same question, "What did you do to better humanity?"

The politician paused for a second and then,

pointing to the pastor and CEO, said, "I gave them tax breaks for lying and stealing."

I'm conflicted when it comes to religions and money. Most secular activists seem to want a complete separation between religions and government and want to remove all the tax benefits religions receive. I, too, have advocated this position and will advocate that approach in this chapter. But the reason why I'm conflicted on this issue is because there isn't much of a precedent for this approach succeeding.

If the goal of secular activism in the United States is to turn the United States into a largely secular society like the countries of Western Europe, then secular activists could theoretically argue for the exact opposite of a separation of religion and government. In Norway and Denmark there is not a separation of church and state like there is in the United States. To the contrary, these countries have state religions that are funded with tax dollars. Clergy for the state churches are state employees. In these countries, religious attendance is very low—less than 5 percent report attending religious services on about a weekly basis—even though large percentages of the populations identify as members of the state religions (~70 percent).

What's the connection between low levels of religious participation and state churches in these countries? While the churches have a prominent position in these countries, they also have much less autonomy than do religions in the United States (though recent legislation grants these churches more autonomy). Historically, the state had a say in who the clergy were going to be. Since these religions rely on tax dollars for funding, that also gives the state control over church policies. If the government legalizes same-sex marriage, guess which religions in these countries are going to have to perform same-sex marriages? If the government mandates gender equality, guess which religions are also going to have to advocate gender equality? Do you see where I'm going? When religion and government are closely integrated, like in Denmark and Norway, the secular state controls religion to a much greater degree. And the result, interestingly, is neutered religion. When was the last time you heard about a Church of Norway pastor trying to burn copies of the Koran? When was the last time you heard about a sexual abuse scandal involving clergy in the Church of Denmark? Close government oversight weakens religion, so long as the government has the upper hand and is secular (if religion has the upper hand, well, that's when you get hunts for atheists, witches, Jews, blacks, women, and queers).

In addition to government being able to regulate religions in these countries, there has been some speculation among sociologists that the close integration of religion and government in these countries has resulted in "lazy monopolies." There is some truth to this idea. Consider a Church of Norway service in contrast to a megachurch service in the United States. Even if you haven't been to either of these, you probably get the idea. Megachurch services in the United States are basically like professional sporting events or concerts. They often have live, upbeat music, huge screens, and charismatic pastors who try really hard to manipulate people's emotions. Do you think Church of Norway services are like that? Of course not. They are typically traditional services that are rather staid. Nothing controversial is taught from the pulpit. And the music would put a cocaine addict on speed to sleep. Why? Whether or not anyone shows up to their services, pastors in Norway and Denmark get paid. But if no one shows up to a megachurch service in the United States, how is the pastor going to pay for his private jet and $6 million home? State-church entanglement like that in Norway and Denmark would substantially reduce the entrepreneurial and economic incentive that underlies religion in the United States.

So, I'm conflicted. A very effective way to reduce interest in religion—an approach that has been shown to be quite effective, even if unintentional—is to tear down the wall between religion and state and closely integrate the two. I'm guessing more than a few readers will have just thought after reading that last line, "Blasphemy! Burn the heretic!" But my point is that this approach actually worked. Religion in Denmark and Norway has been defeated; it is basically the least offensive, most benign, and weakest religion in the world!

But . . .

The United States is not Denmark or Norway. If we were starting the country from scratch and could structure the country any way we wanted, maybe we'd follow the Danish or Norwegian approaches. But we have 200-plus years of post-European-conquest history in the United States with pervasive, pluralistic Christianity. We're not starting from scratch. We've got to figure out how to defeat religion within the present U.S. context. How do we do it?

One approach—nearly opposite to the Scandanavian approach—would be to turn to the invisible hand of the free market and completely deregulate the religious marketplace.

Under this scenario, religion in the United States would be modeled on eighteenth-century laissez-faire capitalism, and pastors would be allowed to say and do whatever they wanted without government regulation. If a priest wants to sacrifice humans and he can find people willing to be sacrificed, let him. If pastors want to have anal sex with their male and female followers—as Jim Jones did—and can convince their followers to give them all of their money—also as Jim Jones did—let them. If rabbis want to endorse political candidates, let them. If clergy want to spew invective against gays, lesbians, transgender individuals, bisexuals, queers, blacks, Hispanics, Asians, atheists, women, etc., let them.

Seriously?

Yes! Seriously!

Of course, some Americans would join such churches as there are some religious organizations that already denigrate most of the groups listed above (particularly sexual minorities, but also atheists): the Westboro Baptist Church, some conservative mosques, some Orthodox Jewish synagogues, etc. Clearly there is a market for hate speech, as the continued existence of the KKK and other white supremacist groups in the United States suggests. But most such groups are marginalized and are explicitly labeled as hate groups. The same could and should be done with religions (see suggestions below). Religious justification for hate should not be seen as an exemption. It's still hate. And anyone bigoted enough to join such a religion would be tainted by that membership. They would be part of a hate group.

But what about the more extreme beliefs and rituals, like human sacrifice? What should be done about that? Nothing!

So long as they are sacrificing someone who willingly and knowingly volunteered, wouldn't they actually be doing the secular movement a service? That'd be one less extremely religious person to worry about! (Note: I say this quite tongue-in-cheek; I'd really hope no religions try to reinstitute human sacrifice.) Of course, there is the concern that religions might prey on those who are not mentally stable. But if they did, the respective clergy could be prosecuted for preying on the vulnerable and sent to prison, which would further remove extremely religious individuals from society. Win-Win!

But what about more benign activities like religions endorsing political candidates? Well, there is pretty good evidence that when religious clergy endorse political candidates, they alienate followers who disagree with them in the process, resulting in people leaving the religion. This doesn't necessarily mean those who leave become nonreligious, but many likely would.

Another benefit of such a shift in policy would be that religions would likely become completely homogeneous—only people who agree completely with the views of the clergy would stick around. As a result, liberal Christians would not attend the same services as fundamentalist Christians (which doesn't always happen, but is pretty common in large religions, like Catholicism). Likewise, liberal Muslims wouldn't attend the same mosques as fundamentalist Muslims. Ditto other religions. Religious fundamentalists would no longer be able to hide behind the more moderate or progressive views of their nonfundamentalist coreligionists. It would be increasingly easy to single out extremist mosques, synagogues, churches, and temples to be labeled as hate groups.

Don't take what I'm saying the wrong way. I'm not arguing that we should target any one particular religious group for discriminatory treatment. To the contrary, I'm arguing that any group that uses religion to justify hatred should be labeled as a hate group. Religion is not an acceptable justification for hate speech, nor is any other meaning system. I don't care if you're a Haredi Jew in Israel inveighing against homosexuals, an extremist Sunni Muslim in the United Arab Emirates inveighing against atheists, or a fundamentalist Mormon in rural Arizona inveighing against gender equality, hate speech is hate speech.

If I'm right, I think something interesting might happen. Religions would likely learn that doing certain things—like endorsing political candidates or denigrating specific groups of people—alienates their followers. The invisible hand of the market—with the help of a broad campaign to label hateful religions as such—could potentially "regulate" religion.

But there's another reason why I'm advocating reduced restrictions on religions. If government doesn't regulate religion, this also means that religions no longer receive any tax benefits from the government. Right now in the United States, there isn't a strict separation of church and state. Religions are (allegedly) regulated in certain ways and, as a result, they receive some tax benefits. Religions are not supposed to endorse political candidates, though many do. Religions are not supposed to donate money to political candidates. And religions can teach most anything, but are restricted from engaging in certain practices, like polygamy and human sacrifice. This is supposed to be a compromise: religions get tax benefits and, in return, they accept government regulation.

If we want to remove the tax benefits, then we also have to remove the regulation.

And what are those tax benefits? Religions pay no federal, state, or local income taxes. Money and tangible assets donated to religions are not taxed. What's more, those who give money or tangible assets to religions get to deduct those "donations" to religions as charitable deductions, which incentivizes people to donate money to religions. Religions also pay no property taxes, capital gains taxes, unemployment taxes, or sales taxes. Religions can also own for-profit enterprises. Some of those enterprises are completely tax exempt, if it can be shown that the enterprise is directly related to the ends of the religion, like book publishing. If the enterprise is unrelated to the religion's ends, they are privately owned and the profits from those enterprises can be donated to the religions, resulting in tax-free income for the religions and significant tax deductions for the for-profit corporations they own. Religions do not have to file income tax returns and have no financial accountability to anyone, as they do not, technically, have shareholders. It's next to impossible to audit religions and their finances are only as transparent as the religions themselves make them. Religions are also the beneficiaries of billions of hours of volunteer labor every year and they can raise money through fundraisers, like bingo or selling used goods. And, of course, federal and state faith-based initiatives result in the direct transfer of billions of tax dollars to religions, though purportedly for secular purposes (all the evidence suggests that this isn't policed in any serious way).

Clergy receive their own tax benefits. They do pay income taxes, but they can reduce their housing costs from their income taxes. This is called the parsonage exemption and includes everything from a mortgage or rent to retiling the pool. Clergy can also opt out of social security taxes, though they won't get social security benefits when they retire. Clergy from all religions are entitled to this benefit: rabbis, pastors, priests, imams, gurus, etc.

There is no easy way to know just how much this special treatment of religion in the United States costs taxpayers, though I did try to estimate this in an article published in *Free Inquiry* and came up with a cost of about $71 billion annually. There are, of course, problems with an estimate of this nature. But the point is that governments in the United States—federal, state, and local—all provide direct and indirect benefits to religions.

How much do these benefits matter? There is no way to know all the ways that religions benefit from these subsidies, but I do have an example that I think is quite illustrative. I attend religious services a couple of times a year just to see what religious people are doing (it's kind of like a biologist going for a hike in the forest). For one of these visits, I attended a Presbyterian service in St. Petersburg, Florida. The service was held in a quaint, old church that could have easily accommodated about three hundred people. About thirty people were in attendance. The average age was over sixty. After the service there was coffee and cake. I stayed after for the treats and struck up a conversation with one of the long-time members. In the conversation that ensued, I asked him how the religion was surviving financially considering the costs associated with maintaining the property had to be quite extensive. He admitted that they were eating through their reserves quite quickly and that the current revenues and reserves were not going to be able to cover their costs in about five years. When I asked him what was going to happen at that point, he shrugged his shoulders.

Now consider the situation of this church in light of the tax benefits it receives. I later looked up the real estate evaluation of the property and it came in at close to $1 million. If the church had to pay property taxes, just property taxes, the church would have shut down decades earlier. And if it also had to pay capital gains tax, income tax, sales tax, and its pastor couldn't deduct his parsonage costs? . . . The benefits religions receive are literally keeping some churches alive. Of course, some religions bring in big bucks, but they are the exception, not the rule.

Step 5 in defeating religions is to cut off their federal, state, and local subsidies. And to justify cutting off these benefits, we also allow religions free reign to be as extreme and bizarre as they want to be. Here are some specific actions you can undertake:

Recommendations for Individual Secular Activists

- Look up your local megachurch pastors and become a private investigator. Since they are public figures, follow them around within the bounds of the law and document their lives. How much time do they spend on their yacht? How much time do they actually spend at church? How expensive is their home? How many cars do they have? How big is their pool? Do they participate in any illegal activities (e.g., speeding, not paying taxes for household help, etc.)? Turn your findings into a documentary and upload it to YouTube. Let's expose the most extreme religious tax abuses.

- If you're not a budding film director, create a blog and become a regular commentator on religious affairs in your local area. Again, follow the "private investigator" model and investigate local clergy—rabbis, imams, pastors, priests, gurus, etc. See what they are really up to. If you have the financial resources, advertise your blog in the local area. And if you write some particularly compelling entries, while being cognizant of relevant libel laws, send them to the local paper as letters to the editor.

- Help out with the "rate how hateful your local churches are" effort one of the national secular organizations begins (see below). If they don't begin one and you have the technical chops to do it, do it yourself.

Recommendations for Local Secular Activist Groups

- Access local property tax records and calculate how much property religions in your local area own and how much it is costing the local government in tax revenue. Write an op-ed for your local paper showing how much religious tax exemptions cost the local community.

- If you have a good lawyer in your group who can defend you from the IRS, start a religion. Then approach your local drug dealers and invite them to launder their money through your "religion." Set each of the drug dealers up as an "assistant pastor" and pay them nice salaries. Services can be parties. And the local secular group will simply take a cut of the revenues. If every local secular activist group in the nation started laundering money for drug dealers, it wouldn't take long before secular activists had the same levels of revenue as do religions. Since religions virtually never get audited, you should be fine. ;) (OK, I'm joking about the money-laundering and law-breaking part, but I'd encourage budding novelists or filmmakers to run with this type of storyline to help call attention to the unnecessary privilege given to religion.)

- Create a clearly fake Twitter account for a hypocritical and hateful clergy person that is satirical. Since it's a lot of work to keep up a fun Twitter account, make it a group effort and give five or six people the ability to tweet. Come up with clear guidelines for how you'll frame the "fake" thoughts of the clergy person, but have fun with it and see how much attention you can draw to his or her lavish lifestyle and vile views.

Recommendations for National Secular Activist Organizations

- Stop trying to get the IRS to police religions when they violate regulations concerning endorsing candidates for office. To the contrary, encourage clergy and religions to endorse candidates. When religions take political positions, they alienate individuals who disagree with their positions.

- Organize a national effort to calculate how much property religions own in the United States and then use those estimates to calculate how much tax revenue is lost as a result. Prepare this as a brief for politicians so religious tax benefits can be part of the discussion of tax reform.

- Organize a national effort to evaluate churches on the basis of how many outgroups they disparage (i.e., create a "hate scale"). If a clergy person and his or her congregation tend to regularly disparage just one or two outgroups (e.g., homosexuals or atheists), then they would get a 2 or 3 on a 10 point "hate scale." (A "0" would be no expressions of prejudice toward outgroups.) At the other end would be Westboro Baptist Church, a congregation that hates basically everyone but themselves (and I wonder about that sometimes). They'd get a solid 10 on the hate scale. Once you've figured out a way to create the rating system for the hate scale, crowdsource a map of local congregations; get help from individual and local secular activists to rate the congregations in their area. The goal would be that any individual in the country could look up his or her local congregation and find out how hateful it is. Oh, and a cool bonus feature would be to create "badges" that correspond to how hateful the congregations are. And a double bonus would be to conduct an advertising campaign with billboards and a Web address inviting Americans to find out, "How hateful is your congregation?"

STEP 6

Encourage Regulated Capitalism

People Would Rather Do Almost Anything Than Go to Church

What's the difference between Disney World and a megachurch?

One's a fantasy land that charges high entrance fees, and the other one has rides.

There are two great ironies when it comes to religion and capitalism. The first is that religion in the United States has increasingly begun to look so much like a capitalist marketplace that it is hard to find ways that the religious marketplace differs from the economic one. They both use slick marketing, they both artificially create demand for products people don't need, they both can be used to make some people very wealthy, and they both compete for consumers. It's particularly ironic because, while religions claim to be morally superior to corporations, I can't think of a single corporation that has filed for bankruptcy because of widespread sexual abuse of customers by the employees.

The second great irony is that one of the most effective tools to defeat religion is, in fact, regulated capitalism. This is ironic because so many conservative religious pastors are staunch advocates of capitalism, not realizing the extent to which capitalism undermines religion. In this chapter, I'm going to focus on the second irony: how capitalism undermines religion. Of course, in light of Step 3, the "capitalism" I'm describing in this chapter is regulated capitalism, not laissez-faire capitalism.

The first step I described to defeat religion—education—is not, unfortunately, for everyone. It's taken me a long time to realize what I'm about to express, but it's a key component of successfully defeating religion: a lot of Americans don't really want to think. They want, instead, for someone else to do the thinking and they want to be entertained.

Now, before you start leveling accusations of elitism at me, let me explain.

I'm a college professor with a PhD. My wife has a PhD. I spend almost all of my time around other college professors who also have PhDs. I started college in 1998, entered graduate school in 2001, and, as of 2014, am still squirreled away in the ivory tower of academia. I also am one of the minority of PhDs who not only received a tenure-track position but also later became tenured. I've spent most of the last sixteen years hobnobbing with people in academia. Most of the people with whom I interact on a regular basis are bright and intellectually curious. When I raise topical issues in pleasant conversation, like what the future of the Arab Spring will be in light of the civil wars and unrest that have resulted, most of the people I spend time with will not only be familiar with the topic but also want to discuss it with me. My friends and colleagues may not agree with me, but they like to ruminate on a variety of topics, from science and politics to art and philosophy. But, as I noted, people like me and my friends and colleagues are not the majority of Americans. We are very much a minority. In 2013, just 3 percent of Americans had doctoral or professional degrees.

The existence of tabloids and TV shows like *Entertainment Tonight* suggest that there is another group of people who are unlike me and my friends. These people don't pay attention to the kind of news I find important. Instead, they are interested in celebrity gossip and fashion trends, as the profits of corporations that cater to these interests attest. These people are also unlikely to be interested in thinking about where they derive their morals, the separation between church and state, or the structure of the economy. They have probably also never heard of scholarly journals or read a peer-reviewed article. Think about it this way: how many Americans do you think could name five living scientists? How many Americans do you think have read a nonfiction book since their last college or high school course? How many Americans know that the modern Thanksgiving story is largely a myth? Or how many Americans do you think can name five countries in Africa or South America?

I'm going to suggest something that may not be polite or politically correct to say, but it is true. These people are *not* intellectually curious. Don't get me wrong. I'm not suggesting that people who are not intellectually curious are in any way inferior to those who are. That's an issue of human worth, and I believe all humans have equal worth. All I'm suggesting is that some people are intellectually curious and others are not. Since you're reading this book, you probably fall into the roughly 40 percent of Americans who are intellectually curious about things like science, politics, the arts, and education.

Why am I bringing this up? Because this lack of intellectual curiosity across large parts of society has implications for defeating religion. For the intellectually curious, education (within and beyond schools) may be sufficient to undermine religion. And as I have argued, we can emancipate women, provide existential security, liberate sexuality, and stop subsidizing religion. But how do we get those who are *not* intellectually curious to stop going to church?

The answer is simple: entertainment. We should encourage capitalists to provide those who are not intellectually curious with alternative forms of entertainment to compete directly with religious services. I'm going to focus on entertainment on Sunday mornings in this chapter, since that is the day when morning entertainment options are particularly curtailed in the United States owing to the predominance of Christianity in the United States, but for other religious holy days (e.g., Friday evening to Saturday evening for Jews; Fridays for Muslims; Saturdays for Seventh-day Adventists, etc.), similar ideas would apply.

The best part about this step in defeating religion is that this entertainment already largely exists, just not at the right time. Sports, movies, and concerts are already widespread, but not on Sunday mornings. I don't think capitalists see the potential benefits of making these forms of entertainment available earlier on Sundays. If you're a capitalist, pay close attention to the following two sentences. Why might you be interested in competing directly with religions? Because there is demand!

I have data suggesting *religious* college students would rather do almost anything than go to religious services. Here's what I did: with a random sample of students from my university and a nearby private university, I singled out the students who reported that they had a religious affiliation and asked them to choose between going to religious services on their respective holy day and doing another activity. I repeated this for more than a dozen different activities. The only activities that lost out to religious services were: playing video games (42 percent chose this over church), watching TV (46 percent), and surfing the Web (48 percent). Religious students at my university would rather do all of the following instead of go to religious services: go to a bar, listen to music, read a book, spend time with a pet, go to a museum, go shopping, exercise, go to a movie, stay home and relax, go out to eat, sleep, go to a professional sporting event, go to an amusement park, go to the beach, spend time with friends, go to a concert, and spend time with family (see figure 3). Of course, these are college students, so I can't generalize from these results to the entire U.S. population. But the results are telling. Basically, religious college students would prefer almost any typical activity over religious services.

I often spend Sundays with my son, and since he gets up fairly early Sunday mornings, I'm usually out of the house by 9:00 a.m. I don't see much traffic. Streets are pretty empty. Starbucks is usually doing fairly well around 9:00 a.m. on

Figure 3. Percentage of Religious College Students Who Would Do Something Other than Attend Religious Services on Their Holy Day

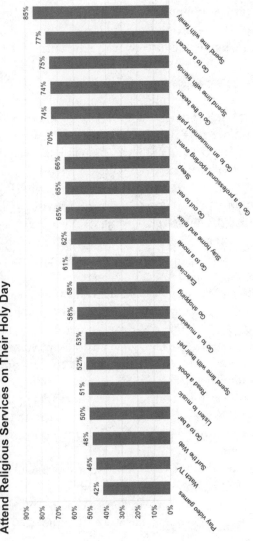

Activity	Percentage
Spend time with family	85%
Go to a concert	77%
Spend time with friends	75%
Go to the beach	74%
Go to an amusement park	74%
Go to a professional sporting event	70%
Sleep	66%
Go out to eat	65%
Stay home and relax	65%
Go to a movie	62%
Exercise	61%
Go shopping	58%
Go to a museum	58%
Spend time with their pet	53%
Read a book	52%
Listen to music	51%
Go to a bar	50%
Surf the Web	48%
Watch TV	46%
Play video games	42%

Source: 2013 Chapel Survey

Sundays, but even our local amusement park, Busch Gardens, isn't very busy Sunday mornings. We held my son's fourth birthday party on a Sunday at 10:30 a.m. and over 90 percent of the people we invited came. We had coffee and homemade zucchini bread for the adults and games for the kids. It was a hit, probably because most parents are looking for things to do with their kids on Sunday mornings.

Now, there is a potential problem with my logic here. How much of the reduced traffic on Sunday mornings is due to people sleeping in from staying up late Saturday night versus people going to church? I don't know. But we do know that only about 1 in 5 Americans is in church on any given Sunday. So, I'm going to guess that the light traffic on Sunday mornings has more to do with people sleeping in or not having lots to do than attending church.

Applying this to corporate America, I wonder how much corporations have thought about this. Is the reason stores open later on Sundays because they believe their target demographic was out late on Saturday, or because they think people are at church? Why does the NFL start Sunday games in the afternoon and not in the morning? Are they worried people won't show up because they were out late Saturday or because they are in church (it could also be to maximize alcohol sales!)? And why don't movie theaters start showing movies at 9:00 a.m. on Sundays, especially family-friendly movies? If movie theaters showed just one family-friendly cartoon every Sunday morning and gave a family discount, I bet they'd make a killing. No matter the reason why U.S. corporations do not open early on Sundays, the end result is self-reinforcing. If they aren't open on Sunday mornings, people won't go on Sunday mornings. And if people are looking for entertainment on Sunday mornings, churches won't have any competition.

So, what's the solution? How can we use this knowledge to defeat religion and at the same time help people make money? Start scheduling things Sunday mornings around 9:00 or 10:00 a.m. Sure, young people who like to party won't be up and about. But think about all of those who are! Most people with kids are up and looking for stuff to do on Sunday mornings. The millions of people who don't stay up late Saturday nights are likely up and looking for something to do. What's more, fewer and fewer of those people are going to church. And, if my students are any indication, many Americans would choose alternatives to church, particularly if they are convenient, cheap, and, most importantly, entertaining.

The point is, people would rather do just about anything instead of attend religious services. Right now, their options are limited on Sunday mornings. I'm fairly confident there is demand for Sunday morning activities. Most church services are boring. A sizable percentage of Americans—perhaps as much as 60 percent—want to be entertained. Give people something more interesting to do on Sunday mornings than church, and they'll do it instead. And capitalists: they'll pay to do it! They are already spending money at church. Why not open your business a little earlier on Sunday mornings to tap into the $100 billion donated to religions every year?

So, what can secular activists do?

Recommendations for Individual Secular Activists

- If you're business-minded, start a business that specifically targets young people on Sunday mornings. Here's just one idea that I'm giving away (mostly for free): start guided running, jogging, or biking groups that meet every Sunday at 9:00 a.m. to explore a new part of town. Plan the routes out in advance. I'm guessing a large number of people would gladly give you the $20 they would have spent at church to safely guide them through parts of their city. Plus, they will get to know other people who like to exercise. If you advertise on dating sites and franchise the concept to the top 20 U.S. cities, I'm guessing this would be a million-dollar company in a year. (And if this works, all I ask in return is an honorary position on your board of directors.)

- Schedule everything you can on Sunday mornings: recreational athletics, birthday parties, play dates. Schedule sleepovers for your kids on Saturday nights so they can play with their friends Sunday mornings. Don't worry—the other kids' parents are pretty unlikely to go to church given that only 1 in 5 Americans do, but you can always check with them in advance. Just make sure you are open about the fact that you won't be going to church first, so they know that you don't expect them to go either.

- Buy your religious relatives who like sports season tickets to a team that plays on Sundays. And if you like sports too, insist on Sunday brunch before every game!

Recommendations for Local Secular Activist Groups

- Since you already have an organized group, use it to help organize other community groups around shared interests that meet on Sunday mornings. Set up a massive monthly game of hide and seek (or some other outside game) in local parks on Sunday mornings. Other options might include: video game or LAN parties for local youth, LARP events in local parks, yoga groups, etc. Basically, anything that can be done Sunday afternoon can be done just as well—and in Florida during the summer with less sweating—on Sunday morning. Bring coffee, and get lunch afterward. And please keep one thing in mind: the target audience is not the intellectually curious, so don't try to make these "events with a message." Don't worry about recruiting people to your secular group. The focus is entertainment and fun. Remember, the goal is to keep people out of church, not necessarily to turn them into secular activists.

- While many secular activist groups are largely made up of intellectually curious people, that doesn't mean you can't also cater to those who like sports. Have Sunday sports parties at a members' house for those who are interested. Start the party around 10:00 or 11:00 a.m. on Sunday, early enough to interfere with religious services. Make sure to invite religious friends. Another option might be to team up with a local sports team, like the St. Paul Saints have done with the Minnesota Atheists, changing their name for a day to the St. Paul Aints. If you can get enough interest, you could get a good discount and may even get good press.

- Engage in letter writing or social media campaigns to get local businesses to open earlier on Sundays. If you succeed, make sure you make it worth their while by frequenting that business.

Recommendations for National Secular Activist Organizations

- There has been a growing interest in professional athletes who "out" themselves as LGBTQ. I'd love to see one of the national-level secular groups sponsor a nonbelieving athlete. You know what I'd love to see just once? An athlete, after he or she wins, say something like, "I'm not giving an imaginary deity any of the credit for this victory. I worked my ass off and had lots of help from real people. They and I deserve the credit." Actually, if you can get a UFC fighter to put your logo on his or her shorts, I'll contribute $50. And if they win and say what I just suggested, I'll double my contribution to $100!

- I'd like to see national secular activist groups approach professional athletic leagues to get them on record saying that they do not discriminate against nonbelievers. It would be pretty cool to see a list of professional leagues that have committed both to being safe places for nonbelievers and to pursuing any allegations of discrimination against nonbelievers.

- National secular activist groups could also work to set up secular groups inside corporations. Many corporations have Bible study groups and other religious groups. Secular individuals should have comparable groups.

STEP 7

Support Education, Art, and Science

Sunday School: Where the questions aren't always dumb, but the answers typically are.

In the previous chapter I argued that secular activists should work toward regulated capitalism because capitalism undermines religion by giving people things to do other than church. Some may find that argument controversial, but now I'm going to suggest something even more controversial. The entertainment opportunities that are likely to result from regulated capitalism will appeal to a sizable percentage of the population, but they won't be of interest to everyone. Why? Because some people aren't really interested in just being entertained. Some people like entertainment that makes them think or find thinking to be their entertainment.

Let's call these people "intellectuals." That isn't a pejorative, even though intellectuals are often disliked in the United States (they can be laughed at, à la *The Big Bang Theory*, but many people don't take them seriously). Many of these intellectuals don't regularly go to professional sporting events because they don't find those events all that appealing, though some do. Intellectuals may watch sports on television or even root for a team, but typically they are a little different in how they think about sports. Intellectuals recognize that professional sports are a pleasant distraction from what they consider truly important in life—the mind. For intellectuals, sports are a means to an end (getting them to not think for a while) rather than an end in and of itself. The nonintellectual sees sports as the end, which is illustrated in how fans identify with teams. Devotion to a team is reflected in some team slogans: "I bleed blue and white" (the Toronto Maple Leafs) or "At some places they play football; at Alabama we live it" (the University of Alabama football team).

Intellectuals are the people who go to the beach and read nonfiction, in the shade, in pants, with sunscreen on, and call it a vacation. They are geeks and nerds. They are oblivious to what is popular, have no idea why people care about the Kardashians or Justin Bieber. They listen to music that helps them think or makes them think, not music that prevents them from thinking (unless they want to not think). To these people, thinking is fun. Thinking is their entertainment.

Now, before you go off and call me an elitist or attack me for suggesting that intellectuals are somehow superior to nonintellectuals or malign me for creating a divide that doesn't actually exist, let me back this up with a little bit of data. There were a couple of questions in the General Social Survey in 2000 and 2002 that I think captured this divide. The questions asked, "In the past 12 months, have you used the Web to do each of these things?" Participants were asked

Figure 4. Percentage of Americans Who Used the Web to Learn about Specific Issues

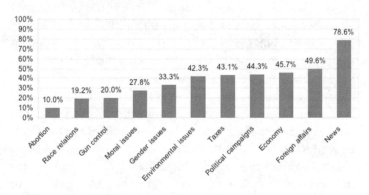

Source: GSS, 2000–2002

about a variety of issues, from investigating race relations to understanding taxes. Figure 4 shows the percentages of people who used the Web to investigate a variety of issues.

With the exception of the news, less than 50 percent of Americans used the Internet to learn about most topics. Granted, there may be a percentage of the population that did not have access to the Internet. But the very high percentage of Americans reporting they had used the Internet to learn about the news suggests that at least that many could have used the Internet to learn about race relations or moral or gender issues, but they didn't. Why didn't they? I believe the answer is that they are simply not curious about those topics.

Don't get me wrong—I'm not saying that nonintellectuals are stupid or don't care about important issues or are any way inferior to intellectuals. In fact, figure 4 illustrates another important point here—intellectual vs. nonintellectual is not a strict line; it's fluid. Some people are more interested in one topic than another. All I'm suggesting here is that intellectuals like to spend a lot of their free time thinking while nonintellectuals would rather spend that time being entertained in ways that mean they don't really have to think.

Why do I bring this up? Well, for-profit corporations tend to target the nonintellectuals for an obvious reason— they make up the majority of people in the United States. As I noted in the previous chapter, for-profit corporations are doing a decent job for the majority of people and could meet demand with slight changes in their schedules. But think about the types of entertainment intellectuals enjoy? They love a good scholarly lecture. They like museums, art galleries, musicals, operas, ballets, and documentaries. They like to read nonfiction.

That intellectuals are a minority can be seen in comparing attendance numbers at museums versus sporting events. In 2014, 111.5 million people watched the Super Bowl; in contrast, the most-visited museum in the United States, the Smithsonian Air and Space Museum in Washington, DC, had about 8 million visitors that entire year. Of course, the Super Bowl is on TV, so the comparison isn't completely fair, but try this: a total of 17.2 million people attended an NFL game during the 2009–10 season. With tickets for an NFL game averaging close to $200 a piece, this suggests that people are willing to pay a lot of money to be entertained, but many fewer are interested in museums, even when they are free.

If secular activists are going to work to bring about

alternative forms of entertainment for those who like to be entertained in nonintellectual ways in order to compete with religion, I think it also makes sense to show some interest in providing forms of entertainment for those who are more intellectually oriented. While the same General Social Survey data suggests that intellectuals are more likely to be nonreligious, there are a fair number of religious intellectuals, too. Creating secular alternatives for intellectuals means religious intellectuals, too, will have something to do rather than think about religion. Intellectuals should be studying philosophy at a university rather than theology at a church or seminary. They should be reading about ethics from leading modern ethicists and discussing it with those ethicists, rather than reading scripture written thousands of years ago that advocates deplorable moral standards. Between the variety of entertainment options provided by for-profit corporations and those provided by universities, civic associations, and art institutions, secular activists should make sure that everyone can find an alternative to religion.

Step 7 in defeating religion, then, is to support, sponsor, and facilitate educational, artistic, and scientific pursuits for individuals who are more intellectually oriented. Having visited and presented to many local secular groups, my impression is that many of the members are intellectually oriented and educationally privileged. The General Social Survey data backs that up, as the percentage of nonreligious people interested in each of the web inquiry topics is higher than the percentage of religious people in just about every category (e.g., 30 percent of religious people are interested in gender issues compared to 47 percent of nonreligious people). The secular activists

I have met like to think and enjoy a good presentation that pushes their intellectual boundaries. If the same holds for most secular activists, then this is really an opportunity to be rather self-serving, since my recommendations will basically suggest that you do things to support activities you enjoy. Here are some things you can do:

Recommendations for Individual Secular Activists

- The next time your alma mater asks you for a donation, tell them you'll donate conditionally. Ask them to use your donation to advertise some of their more prominent lectures publicly. If you've got fairly deep pockets, you could even have an annual lecture named after you and create the criteria for what the lecture is on and how it is advertised.

- If you're a devoted fan of an aspect of the local art scene in your area, start a blog about it. Blog regularly about what is going on. There are two potential benefits here. First, you'll provide advertising for the local art scene. Second, you can weave into your blog secular themes that you see in the arts.

- While there's nothing wrong with donating on Kickstarter, why not help fund science or art? Try Experiment.com or Petridish.org, where you can help fund scientific research. Or why not fundraise for local independent artists or writers?

Recommendations for Local Secular Activist Groups

- If you aren't already doing so, try to advertise your events as widely as possible. Try to target free options, like community newsletters, but local newspapers may also be willing to advertise your events. One of my local newspapers, the *Tampa Bay Times*, has a section of its Web site called "Things To Do." I check it regularly, looking for things to do with my son. I've never seen a secular activity listed in there, but I see lots of religious activities listed. Local secular activist groups should list all of their activities in the local paper, especially if doing so is free.

- If your secular group is musically gifted, why not sponsor some free concerts? I regularly see free choir concerts at churches advertised in my local area, particularly around the holidays. I never go, but I'd consider attending a secular-sponsored concert, particularly around the holidays.

- Organize trips for your group to concerts, museums, and lectures at universities.

Recommendations for National Secular Activist Organizations

- One of the most effective ways minority religious groups have gained legitimacy in academia is through the funding of endowed chairs—academic positions funded by a large endowment (i.e., several million dollars) that helps offset the costs of the position. The beauty of endowed chairs is that those who set up the endowment also get to develop the criteria for the chair. Catholics, Jews, Mormons, and

Muslims have all done this, raising funds to support scholars who are sympathetic to the religion and who then focus their research on the specific minority religious group. National secular activist groups should start raising funds for endowed chairs at universities and use those endowments to hire individuals who study secularism. It will help legitimize research on secular topics. (I have a few ideas for good candidates!)

- National secular activist groups should consider funding research on specific aspects of the secular movement. There is a growing group of scholars, many of whom are affiliated with the Nonreligion and Secularity Research Network (nsrn.net), who are interested in these topics. If you do fund research projects, I'd strongly encourage you to require that the results be published in an open-access journal, like *Secularism & Nonreligion*. Open-access research makes science more accessible to everyone, including intellectuals. Many smaller research projects can be completed for a couple thousand dollars, and scholars would jump at the opportunity to take on such projects, as research funds are limited and very competitive.

- National secular groups may want to consider occasionally advertising in the programs at art events, like ballets, operas, symphony orchestras, and theatrical productions, or in the informational pamphlets at museums that often have maps. Intellectuals are more likely to attend or visit these types of locations, making those ideal locations for recruiting sympathetic individuals.

STEP 8

Syncretize Holidays and Rituals

What do Easter crosses and Easter eggs have in common?

Kids like them better in chocolate.

There has been some discussion among secular individuals about whether holidays and important life event rituals are important or necessary. From what I can tell, views are mixed. Some secular individuals think all rituals and holidays are inherently religious and that they must, therefore, be destroyed, along with religion. As a result, they refuse to celebrate holidays that are laced with religion and try to avoid participation in rituals. Others find such holidays and rituals rather benign and don't believe they are causing much harm, so they participate in them.

I understand that some secular individuals really dislike religious holidays and rituals. I get that. But if you want to defeat religion, boycotting holidays and avoiding rituals is *not* the way to do it. You see, religious holidays and religious rituals are here to stay. People like them. They are a part of every culture. If secular activists want to defeat religion, they should steal a page from the *Catholic Handbook of Conquest*, which doesn't exist, as far as I know, but it should! Catholics were the masters of *syncretism*. If you are unaware of syncretism, you absolutely need to become aware of it. Syncretism is the adoption of religious beliefs or practices from one religion by another religion, usually as the result of contact or conquest. The Catholic Church, as it exists today, is the result of syncretism. The introduction of saints into a quasi-monotheistic religion is the result of syncretic encounters with pagans the world over—both in parts of Europe, in the Americas, and in other countries where the Catholic Church ventured. The customs and traditions associated with Christmas are largely stolen from pagan religions. Christmas trees come from pagans in Germany and Northern Europe; they aren't mentioned anywhere in the Bible. The date for Christmas, also not mentioned in the Bible, was probably based on a holiday that existed among the pre-Christian Romans—*Dies Natalis Solis Invicti*—or Day of the Invincible Sun God. The very name "Easter" is stolen from a pagan goddess, Ēostre. This holiday, celebrated in the spring and later tied to "rebirth" through the association with Jesus's death and resurrection, is also not coincidental as it was originally intended to align with the Jewish Passover.

Why did early Christians syncretize these elements of existing religions? To make the adoption of Christianity easier. You can think about it hypothetically. Let's pretend that Canada invades the United States and miraculously defeats the U.S. military, taking control of the country. With the U.S. conquered, Canada decides to assert its new authority over Americans (i.e., United Statesians), but, smartly, decides not to push things too far. What do they do? Well, Canadians celebrate Thanksgiving in October, not November. So they change the date of Thanksgiving. This introduces change, but allows Americans to keep all of the rituals associated with the holiday. In a more daring and bold move, our new Canadian overlords also decide to institute Boxing Day, which is celebrated on December 26. Since Americans don't celebrate Boxing Day and December 26 is typically the day most Americans spend returning Christmas gifts they don't want, our new Canadian overlords have the brilliant idea of changing the name of the holiday to "Re-Boxing Day" and introduce it as an extension of Christmas; basically, it's the day you "re-box" your Christmas decorations and "re-box" the gifts you don't want. And just like that, Americans get to keep their old Thanksgiving, just on a different day, and have a new holiday connected to Christmas based on a holiday Canadians celebrate. What kind of outrage do you think would result from these subtle changes? Probably not much, because what are Americans out? Nothing, really. We get a new holiday that celebrates what we already do; we just have to call that day something similar to what Canadians call it. The point is, transitioning entire societies into a new belief system is substantially facilitated by absorbing existing belief and practice rather than by forcing wholesale changes in belief and practice.

Pretty much all the major religions have done this. Islam's origins are a combination of pagan, Jewish, and Christian ideas. Judaism drew upon all sorts of other Middle Eastern religions. Hinduism has incorporated literally millions of gods, including Jesus. And Buddhism is not exclusive; you can be a Buddhist and something else—that's how syncretic Buddhism is! Every major religion has evolved through syncretism. Those who want to defeat religion should learn from religions.

The best part about this step in defeating religion is that it is already well under way. In fact, data I gathered from my students in 2013 help illustrate this. I asked my students whether they celebrate Christmas. If they said yes, I then asked them what they do to celebrate Christmas. Their responses are summarized in figure 5.

My students are far more likely to give gifts (99 percent do) than watch biblical Christmas movies (just 24 percent do), which indicates corporate America is winning. But they could certainly use some alternative activities for Christmas Eve other than a Midnight Mass and, given how many listen to Christmas music, secularizing that would be a good idea too (see below).

As just noted, one of the most successful contributors to the secularization of religious holidays is corporate America, which, in the name of profit, has commercialized holidays. The commercialization now associated with most major holidays in the United States has its utility, even if you dislike the crass consumerism that results. In order to maximize the appeal of consumption by attracting the greatest number of shoppers, corporations have denuded holiday shopping of all religious meaning. Santa Claus is far more jovial and conducive to consumption than is a bloody, dying Jesus or even a baby Jesus. And what, really, is the harm in replacing one mythical figure

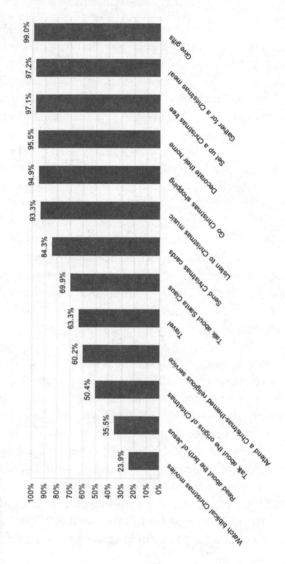

Figure 5. Percentage of My College Students Who Participate in Various Christmas-related Activities

- Give gifts — 99.0%
- Gather for a Christmas meal — 97.2%
- Set up a Christmas tree — 97.1%
- Decorate their home — 95.5%
- Go Christmas shopping — 94.9%
- Listen to Christmas music — 93.3%
- Send Christmas cards — 84.3%
- Talk about Santa Claus — 69.9%
- Travel — 63.3%
- Attend a Christmas-themed religious service — 60.2%
- Talk about the origins of Christmas — 50.4%
- Read about the birth of Jesus — 35.5%
- Watch biblical Christmas movies — 23.9%

with another, particularly when everyone over about the age of eight knows the new one is a myth? Hanukkah is growing increasingly similar to Christmas in how it is celebrated, with the focus shifting to the presents and away from the original meaning of the holiday. Likewise, Easter is, for corporate America, more about bunnies and candy than it is about a dead Jewish zealot who miraculously came back to life. Passover is increasingly more about getting together with family for a special meal than remembering the night Jews in Egypt painted their doors with blood so God would kill only the firstborn of the Egyptians. President Obama has annually celebrated Ramadan with a large dinner, at the risk of reigniting the rumors of him being Muslim. Even Halloween, which is more widely known to have its roots in pagan religion, has come to be a celebration of the dead with its cast of creepy characters thanks, in large part, to Hollywood and corporate America, which are both pursuing money, not indoctrination. So what if jack-o'-lanterns were originally designed to scare away evil spirits? Today, no one thinks of them that way.

The religious, of course, are on to this. Some don't celebrate Halloween because they know of its pagan origins. They regularly fret about the "war on Christmas," which is a bit ironic given its pagan origins. If religious fundamentalists took just a few minutes to learn about their beliefs, they'd realize that they are the ones who should be boycotting Christmas, not secular individuals. Likewise, many religious people want to emphasize the "true meaning of Easter": the crucifixion of one-third of their god and his miraculous resurrection. Of course, this "true meaning" typically doesn't prevent them from decorating pagan-goddess-inspired eggs and encouraging their kids to run around for candy. A similar emphasis among the religiously devout can be seen with Passover and Ramadan as well. In short, corporate America is well on its way to realizing this step, and the religious are, futilely, trying to fight against this.

Atheist activists can help by simply celebrating these holidays in a secular fashion. What might secular versions of these holidays look like? I don't know that any changes are required for Halloween, as it is largely secular. However, I do think returning to the pagan roots to find some meaning for the holiday is not a bad idea. Samhain, the Gaelic precursor to Halloween that was combined with the Roman Catholic Church's All Saints' Day, was a day to celebrate the fall harvest and to remember the deceased. Of course, in the United States (and many other countries), there is a separate holiday, already largely secular in practice though not in origin, that is associated with giving thanks, Thanksgiving (early precursors to this holiday were very much about showing proper thanks to God; today it's more about college football and gluttony, which corporations love). Scientific research has shown that showing gratitude is beneficial for mental health. Thus, Halloween need not focus on giving thanks for the harvest, since that is the focus of Thanksgiving. But why not use Halloween as an opportunity to pause and reflect on your ancestors? This doesn't mean that you have to engage in some practice akin to worshipping them or setting a place for them at dinner, like the Celts did. Personally, I find it humbling to consider that my great-grandfather, Mormon Cragun, spent his entire life working on a farm. In fact, he died on his farm when his tractor rolled over him, pinning him under the tire for hours until his family realized he was missing and sent someone to the orchard to find him. For many humans on the planet today, our lives are much nicer and far more comfortable than were those of our ancestors. Pausing to reflect on that may help ground us to the bounty and beauty that surround us.

Thanksgiving is a bit too gluttonous for me, but I do value the chance to consider what I have and what I am thankful for. I don't know that much should change about how Thanksgiving is practiced aside from encouraging more healthy eating habits and cutting out prayers. Obviously a more accurate history for the holiday should be taught in schools, since the pro-Puritan version is both racist and inaccurate. But if schools want to let kids decorate turkeys around Thanksgiving, what's the problem with that? (Unless you're vegetarian, of course! That said, vegetarian and vegan kids could decorate tofurkeys, and wouldn't that be interesting!)

Christmas, too, is a chance to spend time with friends and family. It need not include presents, though kids seem to really enjoy that part of the holiday. Why not make it about giving, family, and friends and focus on those aspects? I think the myth about Santa Claus should stay for now, to keep the myths about Jesus at bay in kids' minds. It could eventually be combined with Hanukkah (Chanukkah? Hanmas? Hanukkmas?). Trees can easily be decorated with menorahs and giving gifts can be spread over eight days instead of one (or four—compromise and split the difference). Someone should rewrite the "Twelve Days of Christmas" into the "Eight Days of Hanukkah."

I also like the idea of a roaming holiday. Everyone in the West knows when most of the Judeo-Christian holidays are going to be since they are tied to the Gregorian calendar.

But Islamic holidays, for example, shift based on the lunar calendar Muslims employ. Wouldn't it be nice to have a short celebratory holiday that just kind of pops up in a new place every year, perhaps modeled on Ramadan? Rather than a month of fasting, you get three days off from work, have to fast from sunup, and then, when the sun goes down, you have a feast. Stealing an idea from Mormons, the money not spent on lunch could be donated to charity.

Easter is a great opportunity to think about spring and the renewal of life. Let kids hunt for candy and eggs. It's fun and decent exercise, depending on your enthusiasm in hiding the candy. Then have a delicious Passover brunch and spend the day thinking about the future and what you want to accomplish in life. This is another holiday where names could be combined. I prefer Eastover, but Pass-a-Bunny would work too!

There you have it: secular holidays (a term that is, of course, something of a contradiction, considering the origins of the word "holiday"—"holy day").

Holidays from work have been shown to be beneficial for human health and happiness. But what about rituals? When I became an atheist and secular humanist, my initial response to ritual was to reject it. I saw it as a carryover from religion and wholly unnecessary. I was so opposed to ritual after leaving Mormonism that I considered not attending my hooding ceremony when I received my PhD from the University of Cincinnati. My advisor convinced me otherwise by simply suggesting that rituals need not have religious overtones and that they are a useful way to reflect on major transitional milestones in one's life. Attending religious services a couple of times a year (just to observe for my work) has helped drive this point home to me. Ritual activity as simple as regularly allotting time for meditation and contemplation frees the mind from the bustle of everyday activity. In fact, there is evidence that spending time in nature, meditating, and praying all have positive mental health benefits. Additionally, communal ritual, like recitation, is a powerful tool for increasing a sense of unity with others. Speaking or singing in unison can lead to a strong sense of solidarity. Signifying important milestones with simple ritual observances can help people feel a sense of accomplishment and self-worth. None of these activities need include supernatural components. Thanks to various humanist groups, there are already numerous secular rituals to mark such important milestones and events, like the humanist confirmation ceremonies for youth in Norway.

So, what am I suggesting? Step 8 is to syncretize religious holidays and rituals. Take them over. Make them secular. Remove every last vestige of religion. But, and this is important, make them meaningful, appealing, and fun! Here are some specific suggestions to make this happen:

Recommendations for Individual Secular Activists

- Celebrate the major "religious" holidays in a completely secular fashion. Go big! Have a Ramadan feast. Celebrate Passover. Out "Christmas" Christians. Make your house the most festive house on your street, but in a completely secular way. Spread secular holiday cheer everywhere you go. And wish everyone Happy Holidays.

- Get trained as a humanist celebrant through the Humanist

Society. If trends continue, there is going to be a huge demand for humanist celebrants in the future.

- Hire a humanist celebrant for important moments in your life, like getting married or divorced, or moving in with someone. You could also celebrate: getting your first job; having sex for the first time; getting a new car; or becoming a parent. And a humanist celebrant seems in order when a loved one dies. Rituals help us cope with change and transitions. Embrace them.

Recommendations for Local Secular Activist Groups

- If you happen to have talented musicians in your group, rewrite Christmas (or other religious) songs to remove all the religious elements and then record them. Make the recordings and the lyrics available online for free! (Or, if you're really professional, charge for them and fund your other secular activist agenda items.) But there is a very important caveat here. Don't rewrite Christian-oriented songs to make fun of Christians. Make your new versions both beautiful and meaningful. The goal isn't to poke fun; it's to co-opt religion. Just to illustrate, I rewrote "Silent Night" (see the end of this chapter). In my version I didn't really change the focus all that much—it is still about the birth of a child and its relationship with its parents, but it's now a secular celebration of childbirth and parenting and says nothing about Jesus. Who is going to hate a song that celebrates childbirth and parenting? Of course, devoted Christians may hate it because it removes the Christian message. But once my version becomes popular and some famous musicians record it, eventually, everyone will be singing my secular version. And when that happens, secular activists will have truly won the so-called war on Christmas!

- If your local group has talented writers and visual artists, write and illustrate secular versions of holiday stories and make them available online, either for free or, if they are really popular, for a small fee. The point is to create new myths surrounding formerly religious holidays that become more popular than the religious myths. Wouldn't it be great if parents read a really good secular Christmas story on Christmas Eve about a nonbeliever who goes out of his or her way to help someone in the "spirit of Christmas" rather than the Bible story about Jesus being born in Bethlehem (though he was from Nazareth), accompanied by wise men or shepherds, depending on which Gospel you read?

- Come up with a really cool Christmas Eve secular service that people can attend to celebrate Christmas. Market your event widely as a secular alternative to Midnight Mass or other religious services (e.g., call it a "Christmas Eve Mass Action"). You could even combine this with a program like Toys for Tots. Here's what I'm thinking. Start by advertising a toy and food collection program (or working with an existing one) at the beginning of December. On Christmas Eve, have people arrive in the evening to help get everything ready (say, around 5:00 p.m.). You could even make this a joint potluck and service event. After dinner and packaging everything up, break up into groups and deliver toys and some food to the less affluent in your area who have signed up for this service. When everyone is done, return to where you did the packing for coffee, eggnog, and dessert. Combine the coffee and dessert with a reflection exercise in which people get to contemplate why helping others is worthwhile and why Christmas is a good time to do this. A "Christmas Eve Mass Action" would be far more meaningful and humane than a boring sermon and would keep my college students out of church!

Recommendations for National Secular Activist Organizations

- Advertise humanist celebrants. There have been plenty of billboards and bus ads at this point making people aware of the existence of secular organizations and individuals. Now it's time to make them aware of what secular individuals and organizations have to offer them. Take out ads in bridal and wedding magazines, particularly for LGBTQ individuals considering weddings. Take out ads in parenting magazines. Take out ads next to obituaries in newspapers. Here are some suggestions for the ads:

  » For baby-naming ceremony advertisements:

    · Show a picture of a creepy-looking priest who is crossed out. Then have the following: "*We invite kids into the world, not into our pants. Call your local humanist celebrant!*"

  » For weddings:

    · "*It's your day, celebrate how YOU want by saying what YOU want.*"

- · Show a picture of a creepy-looking priest who is crossed out. Then have the following: "*Wouldn't you rather have someone you can trust at your wedding? Call your local humanist celebrant!*"

- » For funerals:

    - · "*Celebrate your loved one's humanity. Call your local humanist celebrant!*"

- The next time Fox News invites a representative from your group on to debate the "war" on Christmas, have your representative show up wearing his or her finest Christmas outfit, bring along a Santa bag, and give every member of the Fox News crew candy canes on live TV! Emphasize all the positive, humanistic ways that you plan to celebrate the holidays. Talk about your favorite secular Christmas stories and carols. The idea is to show viewers that you're having a great time celebrating their *holy day*, in a way that is attractive and appealing. Wash, rinse, and repeat on every major holiday.

- Design attractive, secular Christmas cards for secular activists to send to their friends and family. Not only could you make money selling these, but it's also an easy way to share the secular message.

Original version of "Silent Night"	Secular version of "Silent Night"

Silent night, Holy night
All is calm, all is bright
Round yon virgin,
   mother and child
Holy infant so tender and mild
Sleep in heavenly peace,
Sleep in heavenly peace.
	Silent night, Lowly night
	All is calm, all is right
	Strong is the urging,
	   parents and child
	Cuddle infants,
	   so tender and mild
	Sleep in comforted peace,
	Sleep in comforted peace.

Silent night, Holy night
Shepherds quake, at the sight
Glories stream
   from heaven above
Heavenly, hosts sing Hallelujah.
Christ the Savior is born,
Christ the Savior is born.
	Silent night, Lowly night
	Parents awake,
	   through the night
	Bonds formed
	   through trials of love
	Lullabies sung in the ears of.
	A human child is born,
	A human child is born.

Silent night, Holy night
Son of God, love's pure light
Radiant beams
   from thy holy face
With the dawn
   of redeeming grace,
Jesus, Lord at thy birth,
Jesus, Lord at thy birth.
	Silent night, Lowly night
	Fully awed by love's pure light
	Radiance beams
	   from your lovely face
	With the dawn
	   the night leaves no trace,
	Child, loved at thy birth,
	Child, loved at thy birth.

STEP 9

Change Society to Value Critical Thinking and Scientific Inquiry

> *Three scientists are elected to Congress (that's not the joke). On their first day of the legislative session, they are interviewed by a reporter. The reporter asks each of them what they hope to accomplish during their terms in Congress. The first scientist says, "I'm a climate scientist and would like to see Congress take global warming seriously." The second scientist says, "I'm an energy scientist and would like to see Congress consider alternative energy solutions." The third scientist, pointing to the other two scientists, says, "I'm a sociologist and want to understand why Congress doesn't listen to scientists."*

I have a dream . . .

Okay, I have lots of dreams. But in this dream I ask my college students a question, like, "Is masturbation good for you?" Or, "Who benefits more from heterosexual marriages, men or women?" In that dream, rather than my students responding, "I think X, Y, or Z," one of them will say something like, "Well, I don't know the answer to that, but I'm guessing scientists have investigated it. Let me see what the peer-reviewed, scientific literature has to say!" Then, once we have examined the latest scientific research, we discuss it in class and use these questions to call into question widely accepted beliefs. It's a happy dream because my students would recognize that we can actually try to answer questions using critical thinking skills, empirical data, and scientific inquiry rather than just spouting off opinions.

Right now in the United States, religion is normative. It is widely accepted. When people say they are religious, no one questions that. Of course, if they get specific and mention a religious identity that falls outside the Judeo-Christian mainstream (e.g., Muslim, Mormon, Hindu, Buddhist, Jehovah's Witness, etc.), then people raise an eyebrow. But if you say you're a Methodist, a Catholic, a Jew (Reform or Conservative), a Lutheran, a Presbyterian, a Baptist, an Episcopalian, or even a Pentecostal, most Americans will nod approvingly.

But mention that you're an atheist, and you're unlikely to get the same approving response. Instead, most Americans will immediately think you're immoral. The thought going through their heads is likely something along the lines of, "This person doesn't believe that there is an entity [with characteristics specific to their religious worldview] that is always watching over her. How can I trust that she will behave ethically?" For them, an omniscient god is required for moral behavior. Of course, such an entity is not required for ethical behavior, but that is beside the point—a large percentage of Americans appear to think it is required.

If you try to avoid the prejudice associated with atheism by instead mentioning what you do stand for, say, humanism or freethought, chances are you'll get blank stares. No one is likely to know what you're talking about. Americans have heard of and are afraid of "atheism," but they are unlikely to be familiar with either "humanism" or "freethought." Since "atheism" equals "immoral" in their minds and the other two are unknowns, Americans tend to think quite negatively toward individuals who identify as atheist.

Because religion is normative, religious thinking is also widely accepted. And what does that entail? Religious thinking allows people to arrive at conclusions without evidence and often without even employing logic or reason. Theology may be the worst offender here. As H. L. Mencken noted, "Theology is the effort to explain the unknowable in terms of the not worth knowing." I don't mean to demean the efforts at rigor and logic employed in theology, but it truly is trying to explain the unknowable, which seems pointless to me.

But religious thinking also allows people to arrive at conclusions like:

- Laying hands on someone and praying over them can cure their cancer, hepatitis, AIDS, etc.

- Cows are sacred.

- It's okay to mistreat lesbians, gays, bisexuals, transgender people, and queers because some prehistoric guys said that was okay.

- The earth is 6,000 years old.

- If you're mean to people, you'll be reincarnated as a lesser life-form.

- Pigs are unclean.

- Burning incense helps dead people.

In a related dream to the one I have above, at some point in the not-so-distant future, when someone says, "I believe the earth is 6,000 years old," everyone stops and stares. And then they back away from that person, as though religion and irrationality are contagious. In my dream world, critical thinking, logic, reason, science, exploration, and people are valued, not religion and religious thinking. People would stare at the religious fundamentalist because that person holds a belief that is demonstrably false (and in some ways damaging to society), not because that person is different or a minority. In my dream world, it's perfectly fine to hold beliefs that run counter to the mainstream; believe whatever you want to believe, so long as you are doing your very best to base those beliefs on empirical reality when relevant. When it comes to the age of the planet, empirical reality is relevant. When it comes to issues like how much inequality is acceptable or how much funding the military should receive, empirical reality is still relevant, but the question is open to debate. Wouldn't it be great if the only debates taking place were about topics like that rather than whose make-believe theology is better?

Of course, there are some places where my dream is fairly close to reality. In much of the developed world (e.g., Western Europe, Australia, New Zealand, Japan, etc.), being religious is not normative. And when people say they are religious, that raises eyebrows. In fact, the European Commission asked a sample of Europeans to rank a series of twelve values. Guess which value ranked dead last?

Religion!

This inspired me. I thought it might be interesting to replicate that survey in the United States. Since I don't have the resources necessary to field a nationally representative survey, I had a representative sample of students at my university rank the same twelve values. The results are shown in figure 6.

Religion came in third to last, just above "the rule of law" and "solidarity." I think solidarity was last because students at my university have no idea what it means; there aren't many union activists on my campus ("Solidarity!"). If I had replaced the word with "being united with others in a common cause," I'm guessing it would have ranked higher than religion. Even so, this does suggest two things. First, the devaluing of religion has already taken place at many universities in the United States, and second, the devaluing of religion appears to be well under way among young people in the United States.

Awesome!

Alas, the list of twelve values doesn't include some of the values I'm advocating in this chapter: reason, logic, science, critical thinking, and exploration. But note which values were the most highly ranked: human rights and respect for human life. You know what that tells me? My students are humanists!

But they probably don't know they are.

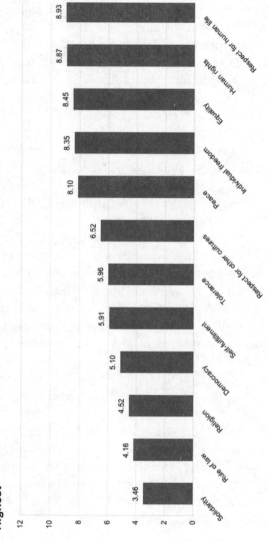

Figure 6. Average Ranking Given by My College Students to Twelve Values, from Lowest to Highest

And that's the problem. I have a younger brother who is a Mormon. In some of our discussions about religion, it would come up that I identify as a humanist and that I hold humanist values. He had never heard of humanism. When I described the values I hold as a humanist, on almost every one of them he would agree with me. He's a humanist. Now that he knows about humanism, he has come to realize that fact. While he still identifies as a Mormon, he also realizes that I am not "just an atheist"; I'm not just what I don't believe, but rather what I do believe. And he agrees with a lot of what I do believe. I think that is probably true of most Americans as well—they share most of the values of humanism, they just don't know it.

So, Step 9 in defeating religion is replacing religious values with critical thinking, scientific inquiry, and humanistic values. Below are some specific actions people can take to change what Americans value. Note that I'm keeping one of these in reserve, as it is the focus of the next chapter—teaching humanist values in school.

Recommendations for Individual Secular Activists

- Wipe "god" from your vocabulary. Don't ever say, "Thank God!" or "Oh my God!" Using these phrases reinforces cultural norms favoring religion. If you find yourself wanting to say "Thank God!" why not try one of the following instead:

  » "Oh my dog!" (If someone gets upset over replacing "god" with "dog," you can always claim dyslexia—no offense to individuals with dyslexia intended.)

  » "Thank probability!"

» "Oh my!" (Ideally said in the manner of George Takei)

- When people ask you what your religion is, tell them "humanism" rather than "atheism" or "none." Of course, humanism is not a religion (though courts recognize it as such now), but saying you are a humanist will likely intrigue people, which will then open them up to discussing what you do believe, not what you don't believe. (If a surveying company or an academic asks you on a survey what your religion is, please feel free to say "none." But saying "none" to friends, family, or random people on the street won't start a conversation about humanism, will it?!?)

- Carry pass-a-long cards that you can hand to people when they ask you what humanism is, ideally that include a link to a Web site about humanism that one of the national humanist or secular groups has created (see below).

Recommendations for Local Secular Activist Groups

- Create T-shirts that celebrate critical thinking, science, reason, logic, and humanism rather than T-shirts that denigrate religion. Tell people what you're for, not what you're against. I'm not getting any kickbacks for this, but one of my favorite Web sites for geeky science clothes is ThinkGeek.com; they have lots of fun shirts that celebrate both science and quirky critical perspectives (and a lot of science fiction). But feel free to come up with your own designs. Just make sure you're careful in creating shirts that don't draw on any outdated ideas that were oppressive to minorities (see Step 2).

- Organize groups to present at local fairs or events and arrive with the professionally produced pass-a-long cards and fliers that the national secular activist groups have produced (see below).

- Hold public celebrations of Darwin Day or celebrate other birthdays of famous critical thinkers or contributors to scientific inquiry and equality, like A. Philip Randolph. I'm suggesting this only in the sense that the goal is to change society so it values critical thinking and science and not religion. Of course, don't turn science into a religion; it should not be treated that way. Celebrate what science can offer as a method of inquiry, without celebrating scientism.

- BONUS: Start the "I'm glad I'm not a fundamentalist campaign." Get ex-fundamentalists to describe something irrational they used to believe or do and end each video with, "I'm so glad I'm not a fundamentalist anymore." Create this channel on YouTube. If it goes viral, your local group could make good money!

Recommendations for National Secular Activist Organizations

- Create expertly produced pass-a-long cards and fliers that local secular activist groups can pass out that detail the key values of humanism. I'll help you. The title should be: *"You're a humanist! Find out why."* Follow that up with a list of the key values of humanism and a Web site people can visit to find out more.

- Speaking of Web sites, do you realize that the URLs humanism.com and humanism.org have nothing to offer about humanism? As of March 2014, humanism.com is parked by Digimedia.com and humanism.org resolves to theworldmarch.org. Seriously, WTF? Everyone on the planet should be able to search for "humanism" and immediately arrive at a Web site in their language that details what humanism is. Most religions have done this, but the secular movement has not. Right now, for me, Google returns the Wikipedia page on humanism as the top item; the American Humanist Association's Web site (americanhumanist.org) comes up second. This is a marketing failure by the secular movement!

- Create a Web site or app that rates politicians based on how fundamentalist vs. secular they are. Build into the system the ability to donate to secular politicians.

- BONUS: I have one last dream—a cable TV channel dedicated to the secular movement (American Atheists had a similar idea with Atheism TV, which they launched in 2014 on Roku). Obviously it would take money to get it started, but it could eventually turn into a money generator. Ideally, it would be a nonprofit that is owned by a secular coalition so any excess revenue could be funneled back into the secular movement. Here's my dream lineup:

Time	Program
6:00 am–8:00 am	Title: *Morning News for Nones*
	Description: Morning news with an atheist/skeptical perspective
	Hosts: Hugh Laurie and Cara Santa Maria
8:00 am–9:00 am	Title: *Secular Living*
	Description: Knockoff of *Good Morning America* that is a bit lighter than the news, focusing on practical ways to improve the lives of all people (e.g., practical parenting advice based on the latest scientific research); definitely no celebrity gossip, though perhaps the show could occasionally host freethinking celebrities
	Hosts: Dale McGowan and Greta Christina
9:00 am–10:00 am	Title: *Science, Because It's Awesome!*
	Description: Science news show; a cool experiment every day to illustrate science, but mostly a summary of the latest research findings from all areas of science
	Hosts: Neil de Grasse Tyson, Bill Nye, and Luke Galen
10:00 am–11:00 am	Title: *Scripture and the Middle East*
	Description: Tackles different topics each day in-depth, providing scholarly insights into the history of scripture and the culture in which Western religions originated
	Host: Bart Ehrman

11:00 am–12:00 pm	Title: *Health and Medicine for Skeptics*
	Description: Describes the latest findings in medicine and health
	Host: Steven Novella
12:00 pm–1:00 pm	Title: *Freethought News*
	Description: News hour with a specific focus on news relevant to the nonreligious
	Host: Hemant Mehta
1:00 pm–2:00 pm	Title: *Skepticism and Feminism*
	Description: Talk show on skepticism and feminism with guests
	Host: Rebecca Watson and Annie Laurie Gaylor
2:00 pm–3:00 pm	Title: *Discussing Religion*
	Description: Examines all kinds of religion; daily guest from a particular religion to examine beliefs, values, commonalities, ways to collaborate, etc.
	Host: John Shook
4:00 pm–5:00 pm	Title: *The Julia Sweeney Show*
	Description: Talk show with guests; knockoff of Oprah, but without all of the pseudoscientific and religious garbage
	Host: Julia Sweeney

5:00 pm–6:00 pm	Title: *Evening News for Nones*
	Description: Roundup of the daily news with the same atheist/skeptical perspective as *Morning News for Nones*
	Host: Jeremy Clarkson
6:00 pm–7:00 pm	Title: *The History of Freethought*
	Description: Examines the history and development of atheism and freethought around the world
	Hosts: Susan Jacoby and Jennifer Michael Hecht
7:00 pm–8:00 pm	Title: *Real Paranormal Investigations*
	Description: Show that investigates paranormal and pseudoscientific claims, but by a real skeptic
	Host: Joe Nickell
8:00 pm–9:00 pm	Title: (Up to the producer, but I'm sure it will be great)
	Description: Original comedy series
	Producer: Ricky Gervais
9:00 pm–10:00 pm	Title: (Again, up to the producers, but this would be amazing, too)
	Description: Original sci-fi series with clear atheism/skepticism themes
	Producers: Brannon Braga, Ridley Scott, or James Cameron

10:00 pm–11:00 am	Title: *Darkside*
	Description: Late-night variety show.
	Host: Tim Minchin
11:00 pm–12:00 am	Title: *Finest Hour*
	Description: Late-night variety show
	Host: Patton Oswalt
12:00 am–1:00 am	Title: *Toward the Singularity*
	Description: Show about futurism, science fiction, and other speculative ideas rooted in skepticism and science.
	Hosts: Michael Vassar and Anne Lise Kjaer
1:00 am–6:00 am	Reruns of: Movies—fiction and documentary—that would appeal to a freethinking/skeptical audience; *Mythbusters* reruns; *Bullshit* reruns; George Carlin and other atheist/freethinker comedy routines

STEP 10

Teach Humanist Ethics in School

What's the difference between secular ethics and biblical ethics?

Secular ethics teach kids how to treat others while biblical ethics treat everyone like a kid.

Have you heard of the "wedge" strategy? This was an idea developed by creationists—who lost in the courts when the courts decided creationism wasn't science—to get religion and creationism back into the public schools. They created the idea of "intelligent design" with the specific aim of getting religion into the schools by "wedging" open the door. They created campaigns like "Teach the Controversy" and pushed the idea that alternatives to evolution should be allowed in biology classrooms. All of this was cover for their real aim— trying to keep young people from learning about evolution, since they are afraid accepting evolution will undermine their fundamentalist indoctrination.

While their wedge strategy failed in the courts (but has

been advocated by various state legislatures), I kind of like the idea of a "wedge" strategy. Here's a wedge strategy for secular activists: advocate teaching ethics in public schools. Public schools already teach values, though most of these are taught indirectly through how course material is discussed and framed. For example, by depicting the United States as a great and powerful country driven by its capitalist economic engine, communism is indirectly depicted as a complete failure and a horrible economic system. Since the Soviet Union collapsed, clearly capitalism is superior (conveniently ignoring the remarkable growth of communist China, which is part communist and part capitalist). Now, I'm not arguing for or against communism here. I'm simply pointing out that communism is typically denigrated in American public education implicitly, if not explicitly. We teach values in schools, even if we don't have a course on ethics or values.

You might be asking yourself: do we need to teach ethics in schools? I think we do for three reasons. First, a very simple way to defeat religions is to completely remove one parental justification for sending kids to church: parents want the churches to teach their kids morality. Given the track records of religions when it comes to morality—sex abuse scandals, embezzlement, opposition to equality for racial, gender, and sexual minorities, killing the Equal Rights Amendment, etc.— religions are the last place parents should be sending their kids for instruction on morality.

Second, one of the major concerns most theistic-leaning people in the United States have about atheism is that they equate it with immorality. As previously noted, many Americans don't trust atheists because they worry that people will behave immorally without an omnipresent god watching over them. If atheists came out in favor of teaching ethics, that might help reduce this distrust.

Third, while this book is primarily about defeating religion, I have to admit that I have other concerns as well related to our present culture. One of them is a growing trend toward a specific type of hedonism. Don't get me wrong; I very much enjoy pleasure. But the way hedonism is manifesting disturbs me. It was fairly well depicted in a 2014 Vice.com article titled "This American Bro: A Portrait of the Worst Guy Ever." Basically, the article describes a caricature of young men who exist solely as tributes to their own self-existence. They drink because they deserve to get drunk. They treat women as objects of their pleasure. They are inconsiderate of others because the world exists for them. They denigrate gender, sexual, and racial minorities to elevate themselves. To them, life is just about making themselves feel good, and if you can't contribute to them feeling good, you are worthless. They exist to celebrate themselves. As a college professor, I see a lot of these young men in my classes, but also a lot of young women who behave in a similar fashion. I have no real sense of how pervasive this perspective is, but it is not conducive to an egalitarian, modernized, progressive world where people—all people—are treated with dignity and respect. In fact, it's the antithesis of that. Why are these people behaving this way? It's likely that they have simply taken U.S. gender norms to their extreme. For white men maybe it's a way to compensate for threats to their "manhood" because white men have been losing some of their dominance and power. Women participate, despite degrading themselves in the process, because cultural norms in the United States support women being submissive and subservient to men. While Step 9 was to change cultural values, I think Step 10 could also help address this growing, inward-looking, self-serving hedonism as well.

So, what should secular activists do? Develop school curricula on ethics for every grade level in consultation with ethicists and leaders of minority rights groups. Now, there are a variety of perspectives on ethics, and I am likely to support teaching any ethical system that teaches tolerance, equality, and the value of critical thinking and scientific inquiry. But this is a guidebook for secular activists, so the obvious choice would be to teach humanist ethics. Courses should teach secular humanist values like those depicted in the Humanist Manifestos, but the courses themselves could be called something like "Universal Values Education" or "Values for the Modern World," a title that is vague enough to cover the content and also hide the secular humanist nature of the values (remember, this is a "secret" guidebook for secular activists). Since the instruction of values should begin at the earliest possible ages, the first set of lessons should target five- and six-year-olds just starting school.

My son, Toren, is four and in preschool. I've already seen a number of illustrations of how he is being taught specific values in his school. For some reason—probably because my wife and I let him watch shows that are rated PG and PG-13 (and occasionally R)—my son has a fascination with guns. After he persistently asked for some, we finally relented and bought him some toy guns (no real guns). But even before we bought him guns, he turned everything he could into a gun. We bought him Legos and, literally, the first thing he built was a Lego gun. He would find sticks whenever we were outside and turn those into guns. He would even take sticks used for stirring coffee at Starbucks and turn those into guns. Thus, we weren't all that surprised when we found out that he picked up a stick at his preschool during outside time and pretended it was a gun. Given the number of school shootings in recent years, Toren's behavior was clearly unacceptable. His teacher pulled him aside and told him he couldn't pretend to shoot the other kids. I can't say that Toren is a genius, but he's also not stupid. He thought about what his teacher was telling him, then told her, "But I'm pretending it's a squirt gun that shoots water." His teacher couldn't tell him that it was wrong to pretend to squirt kids with water, so he got to pretend his stick was a squirt gun.

My point in telling this story is that our schools already teach values: pretending to shoot other kids with a gun is unacceptable. My son has been taught all of the following values already: take turns, don't talk when the teacher is talking, raise your hand to be called upon, clean up after yourself, don't hit, don't push, say "please" and "thank you," shut the bathroom door when you're going potty, and don't bite. I'm not necessarily saying these are values with which I agree. I've talked to Toren about physically defending himself when necessary and, at home, we don't typically close the door when we're changing our clothes, bathing, or using the toilet as we don't want our son to feel ashamed about being naked. My point is, he's already learning values. So, why not teach him and all kids values? And the sneaky, wedge-strategy part is: why not make those values implicitly secular and humanistic (or part of some other ethical system that supports similar ideas)?

Rather than give suggestions for individual secular activists, local secular groups, and national secular organizations in this chapter, I'm going to illustrate how humanist ethics could be taught in schools. Here are seven values, based on Humanist Manifesto III, that could be taught with simple lessons:

1. Knowledge of the world is derived by observation, experimentation, and critical thinking.

    a. *Lesson plan for kindergartners*: Actually use these values to explore the world around them. Ask students to observe similarities between different species (e.g., similar eyes among mammals, birds, and reptiles). Use observation and critical thinking to explain why they might have similar eyes.

    b. *Lesson plan for high school students*: In a quarter- or semester-long ethics class, this value could be the focus for a week or two. Break the students into groups. Each group will choose a topic of interest that can, in fact, be illustrated using observation, experimentation, and critical thinking (e.g., evolution vs. creationism, vaccines don't cause autism, etc.). The groups will debate for the side of observation and experimentation, while the teacher will debate based on faith, emotion, and pseudoscience. The rest of the class will decide who wins each debate. The teacher will intentionally play the part of the foil. Social psychological research has shown that, when you ask someone to defend a position, they often tend to end up believing the position. So, never let the students take a position we don't want them to actually believe.

2. Humans are an integral part of nature, the result of evolutionary change, an unguided process.

    a. *Lesson plan for kindergartners*: Create a cute cartoon video that clearly and accurately illustrates the evolution of humans and explains how natural selection influences which random mutations are selected. Explain at the end why knowledge of human evolution is important: for example, it helps us understand that all humans are one species with common ancestry, addressing specific topics like how different groups of people have evolved different skin colors in order to undermine racist beliefs and values.

    b. *Lesson plan for high school students*: Part 1: Put students into groups and have them discuss then write a paper on what they think the world would be like if there were no humans. Discuss the papers as a class. Part 2: Ask students why it is important to understand that humans evolved (don't even engage on issues of creationism; take human evolution as a given). Discuss some of the important reasons why human evolution is important as a class.

3. Ethical values are derived from human need and interest as tested by experience.

    a. *Lesson plan for kindergartners*: A simple illustration of how values are derived based on need and experience could be illustrated by teaching kids about the difference between appropriate and inappropriate activities based on the environment they are in. Discuss the difference between "inside" and "outside" voices and talk about why it is okay to behave differently in different situations. This will lay the foundation for understanding that what is right and what is wrong is context specific later in life.

b. *Lesson plan for high school students*: Ask students some tricky questions: Is it always wrong to lie? Is it always wrong to kill? Is it always wrong to steal? Have each student come up with five situations in which it is morally appropriate to lie and five situations when it is morally wrong to lie (ditto with killing and stealing). Have them discuss each of these in a group with several other students. If there are any situations where the group is confused or uncertain as to the correct answer, discuss the question as a class.

4. Life fulfillment (can) emerge from individual participation in the service of humane ideals. (Note: I don't think this is the only way people can find life fulfillment, but it's one of the values from Humanist Manifesto III. I modified it somewhat to reflect my views.)

a. *Lesson plan for kindergartners*: While "adjusting" the behavior of kids who behave in ways that are not conducive to a positive learning environment is important, students should also be rewarded and even singled-out for behaving kindly toward others. Tell the kids at the beginning of every week that you are going to be looking for instances in which the kids exhibit a specific positive behavior (change it every week), like: asking for things politely, helping someone who has dropped something, apologizing, saying "thank you," etc. Whenever a student is observed doing one of these nice things, make note of it publicly. It will begin to illustrate to the students that one of the rewards for being humane is a good feeling, which translates into fulfillment.

b. *Lesson plan for high school students*: Have the students choose a volunteering opportunity. Have the students volunteer collectively and process how they felt after volunteering. Highlight the importance of treating others, particularly those who are less fortunate, with dignity and respect and illustrate that there is an intrinsic reward in helping others.

5. Humans are social by nature and find meaning in relationships.

a. *Lesson plan for kindergartners*: Every day for two weeks, pair each child up with another child in the class—a different one each day. Have them do two things: find something they both like and draw a picture of what they like about the other child. Display the pictures each day, then send them home with the kids.

b. *Lesson plan for high school students*: With the help of the students in the course, map out the social cliques and groups in the school using the ideas behind social networks. Make sure every student in the class is on the map (even if someone in the class is not socially connected). Every day for two weeks, take ten minutes of class time and pair two students who do not typically belong to the same social cluster and have them talk, focusing on things they like and common interests they share. At the end of the two weeks, have each student write a short paper on what they learned about groups, people, and relationships.

6. Working to benefit society (can) facilitate individual happiness. (Note: Again, this value needed to be modified slightly as there are other ways to "maximize" individual happiness.)

   a. *Lesson plan for kindergartners*: Have the students create pictures and messages for elderly people in a retirement community. Send the pictures and messages to the elderly. Then have the kids go to the retirement community and meet those who received their pictures and messages and sing them a couple of songs. After the students return, discuss how they think what they did made the elderly feel.

   b. *Lesson plan for high school students*: Discuss with the students what it means to "benefit society." Talk about specific, actionable ways that the students can benefit society (e.g., repairing a playground, changing tax policy to benefit the less affluent, equalizing educational opportunities such that everyone has equal opportunities even if they do not have equal skills or abilities, etc.). Have the students develop a specific plan to benefit society and help them undertake that plan. Once it is complete, discuss why they think working to benefit society can increase individual happiness.

7. Respect for differing yet humane views in an open, secular, democratic, environmentally sustainable society.

   a. *Lesson plan for kindergartners*: In consultation with the students' parents, have each student describe a tradition that is practiced in their home in front of the class. Discuss why that tradition is important to the family and talk about different cultural traditions around the world.

   b. *Lesson plan for high school students*: Break the students up into groups and have them investigate different countries that have cultures that are believed to be quite different from their own. Their goal is to find a cultural tradition that they really like that is not practiced in their own culture but that they think should be (e.g., wearing a surgical mask in public when you are sick like they do in Japan). Talk about why different countries have different cultural traditions and views and how understanding these views can make us more accepting and tolerant of people who seem to be different from us.

CONCLUSION

You know what the best way to defeat religion is?

Together!

One of the local secular groups in my area hosts a Darwin Day event. Since I tend to be rather animated as a speaker, this group has invited me to speak at the event in consecutive years. The first year I shared the stage with Sean Faircloth, author of *Attack of the Theocrats!*. The second year I was the warm-up speaker for Daniel Dennett. After Dennett concluded his presentation, he and I, along with the one other speaker, all sat down as a panel and fielded questions from the audience. One of the questions I regularly am asked when I speak to secular groups is something along the lines of, "What can we do to defeat fundamentalist religion?" Someone asked this of the panel at the Darwin Day event. Dennett and I largely agreed on this, but we emphasized different points. His point, which is likely accurate, was that he didn't think we had to do all that much. The natural processes of secularization (i.e., declining religiosity in the face of modernization) were eventually going to win. I believe he's probably right. That's largely what happened in Western Europe and Australia, New Zealand, and Canada. But it can be a long, drawn-out process. My suggestion was that secular activists may be able to help secularization along, and I suggested a couple of the items in this book as good starting points. Dennett agreed with me and said that it couldn't hurt to help it along.

The suggestions I have outlined in this book are aimed at doing just that: helping speed up secularization in the United States. I have focused on the United States because it is the country with which I'm the most familiar, but that doesn't mean these ideas couldn't be applied elsewhere. In fact, some of them already have been. Norway, for instance, has a very well-developed system of humanist education, including a humanistic confirmation ceremony that includes a course in philosophy and ethics for adolescents. I borrowed this idea for Step 10, teaching humanist ethics in schools. I obviously borrowed the ideas of extensive social safety nets from other modern countries that have these in place. So, it is not just that some of these steps *could* work in other countries, it is that they *have* worked in other countries.

Part of the reason I wanted to write this book is because there is scientific evidence to support most of these ideas. Given the proclivity toward scientific thinking among secular activists, I thought they might want to know what the latest social scientific findings are. Many of the steps I suggest for defeating religion are rooted in the social science of religion and are based on research that examines correlates of secularization. Steps 1 through 6 are all based on either my own research on this topic or related research by other scholars.

Steps 7 through 10 are more geared toward filling in holes in social and civic life that may exist as religion is defeated.

I have also tried, throughout this book, to make clear that speeding up secularization in the United States is something that secular activists can do at multiple levels. Just because you are not on the board of directors of one of the national organizations—American Humanist Association, American Atheists, Council for Secular Humanism, Freedom From Religion Foundation, among others—doesn't mean there is nothing you can do to help. As I noted in the introduction of the book, defeating religion is going to be most effectively accomplished by changing the culture around the religious rather than by trying to change the religious themselves. Simple things, like not referencing Jesus or God unless you also reference a clearly mythological deity in the same sentence, will go a long way toward changing U.S. culture. Being secular needs to become the norm; being a religious fundamentalist needs to become deviant. We need to sever any sense of legitimacy religious fundamentalists currently have in society to defeat religion.

Individual secular activists and local secular groups have a role to play in defeating religion in the United States, just as the national organizations have done and continue to do. The most effective way to defeat religion really is by working together. As more and more Americans distance themselves from fundamentalist religions, it is going to become increasingly normative for people to not be religious. And where religion used to fill a hole in someone's life, secular activists should be ready to offer alternatives: humanist celebrants, humanist philosophy, secular groups for socializing, etc. Together, secular activists can help speed up secularization.

I love sitting around talking about the failings of fundamentalist religion with others who share my views. I also enjoy talking about humanism and the future potential of humanity. But I also think there are some things we can do to make those ideals reality. My hope is that this book will give individuals, local groups, and national organizations some specific actions they can undertake that will help the movement. If you aren't a member of a local or national secular organization, you should join one (or more than one, if you have the time and resources). The national organizations have fought and continue to fight to normalize being nonreligious in the United States. They can use your support. Local groups can be powerful sources of change in the community and can also be an excellent source of support for secular individuals who feel isolated. But even if you want to work alone, there are things you can do. With these ten steps, the only thing you'll have to decide is where to start.

NOTES

To make the book easier to read for those who are not interested in references and citations, I have opted to include notes for the chapters at the end of the book. The notes are organized by chapter and then, within chapters, in the order in which the points that require clarification occur.

Introduction
Sociologists have a pretty clear sense of what we mean when we use the words "fundamentalist" and "fundamentalism." For us, religious fundamentalists are individuals who fail to put their scripture into context and therefore interpret it as the literal words or thoughts of a supernatural entity. Additionally, religious fundamentalists tend to think in black and white—for them, there is only truth and error, and nothing in between (Emerson and Hartman 2006; Antoun 2008). In contrast to religious fundamentalism, there are some religions and some religious people who contextualize scripture and see parts of it (or most of it) as metaphorical (Cragun 2013a). I explain these distinctions in greater detail in my earlier book, *What You Don't Know About Religion (but Should)*. Some liberal religions are actually quite accepting of modern scientific findings, which is part of the reason why they are called "liberal" religions (Cragun forthcoming). As science made discoveries or developed ideas that contradicted

their religious beliefs, liberal religions and many of the members of those religions reformulated their beliefs to take scientific findings into account. Fundamentalism was a response to the liberalizing trend in some religions.

Some of the earliest research in sociology when it was first developing focused on religion (Durkheim 1995; Weber 2001; *The Marx-Engels Reader* 1978). One of the first to note the functions of religion was Emile Durkheim (1995), though others have conceptualized religion in a similar fashion (Bade and Cook 2008). Marx was not the first to suggest that religion can be used as a tool to control others (Cady 2010), but he may have the most famous phrase making that point, "Religion is the sigh of the oppressed creature, the heart of a heartless world, and the soul of soulless conditions. It is the opium of the people. The abolition of religion as the illusory happiness of the people is the demand for their real happiness" (*The Marx-Engels Reader* 1978). Social scientists have also long known that religion contributes to prejudice, particularly toward people who hold values or engage in practices that run counter to those of the religion (Allport 1979; Cragun and Sumerau forthcoming).

That morality can be based on secular philosophy really doesn't need a citation, but some have made this point quite clearly (Cliteur 2010). Weber noted that religion can be used as a basis for deriving authority (Bendix 1978). There are a number of scholarly sources that compare religiosity outside the United States, showing that some countries are much less religious on average than is the United States (Norris and Inglehart 2004; Zuckerman 2006).

In some ways, my previous book (Cragun 2013a) was an attempt to refute an apologist for religion, Rodney Stark, who has argued that religion is a net positive for society (Stark 2013).

The article from *Wired* on apocalypses was pretty interesting, and also appropriately noted that most of the potential apocalypses are highly unlikely (Ridley 2012).

When I suggest that religion is an already weakening element of society, I am referring to the evidence for secularization theory. There is plenty of evidence to suggest that religion is declining as far as the number of adherents to religions and its influence in society go, though the specifics are nuanced (Norris and Inglehart 2004; Bruce 2013; Bruce 2002).

Throughout the book I refer to the movement made up by individuals attempting to normalize nonreligion and nonbelief in the United States as the secular movement, and here I use the word "secular" as an umbrella term that includes all those who work toward this end, whether they self-identify as secular, atheist, humanist, freethinker, or some combination of these terms, or whether they prefer some other term entirely. In some of my academic writing I use the acronym SHAF to refer to secularists, humanists, atheists, and freethinkers. One advantage to an initialism/acronym approach for this movement is that, unlike the LGBTQ+ initialism, many of the words that are the source of the initials can be thought of in two ways. For instance, there are "atheists" and there is "atheism." Atheists are those who have adopted Atheism. I don't think this works with "gay" and "gayism." But with SHAF, it could refer to the people, as in "secularists, humanists, atheists, and freethinkers," or it could refer to what those people espouse, as in "secularism, humanism, atheism, and freethought." One could also tack a "+" on the end of the initialism in order to include any individuals or ideologies that belong in the movement that feel left out (e.g., agnostics and agnosticism). While there are still some people debating whether this is a movement (LeDrew 2012; LeDrew 2013), I think it's time to move past that. It is a movement. It doesn't exactly have a name, but it is a movement. I'm not trying to suggest that SHAF should become the de facto standard initialism. Honestly, my impetus for using the initialism elsewhere was that I got tired of writing out all of the groups of people involved. And if I got tired of writing out all the groups, I was positive that people would get tired of reading all the groups in my effort to be inclusive.

There is a large body of research on how people think and how difficult it is to change people's minds (Haidt 2013). It is precisely because it is so difficult to change people's beliefs and views that I'm suggesting we work around the religious rather than confront them directly. Others have suggested a similar approach (Eller 2010).

For a detailed discussion of what religions are, how they are socially constructed, and how they become a shared reality, there is no better work than that of Peter Berger (P. L. Berger and Luckmann 1967; P. L. Berger 1990).

The Rochester-based "Better News Club" has generated national news coverage. For a balanced piece, see the reporting of Kimberly Winston (2015).

Step 1: Promote and Defend Secular Education
As noted in this chapter, one of the primary functions of education is to educate the workforce, though there are other functions (Pulliam, Van Patten, and Pulliam 2013). However, educating the workforce may not have been the primary justification for developing a system of free public education in the United States in the first place. There is pretty good evidence that the justification was actually based on finding something for the growing number of unemployed kids to do with their time, since they were increasingly not allowed to work in factories, even though they had at the beginning of the industrial revolution. Additionally, individuals in higher social classes felt a moral obligation to help those who were disadvantaged (Katz 1976). Thus, educating kids was more about keeping young people busy—so they wouldn't engage in deviant behavior—and out of a moral obligation to the poor than about educating the workforce.

The numbers of workers in agriculture comes from the Statistical Abstracts of the United States, which were prepared by the U.S. Census Bureau (2012). Specifically, I drew on the 1800, 1900, and 2000 Statistical Abstracts.

For an excellent history of the evolution of the family and the creation of adolescence, see the work of Stephanie Coontz (1992).

There is an extensive literature on attempts to assimilate Native Americans into the culture of their oppressors—whites of European descent (Hoxie 2001).

A culture of consumption isn't innate; it has to be taught. Early sociologists noticed this trend that dovetailed with the industrial revolution—if our industrialists are going to mass-produce goods, they need people to buy those goods (Veblen 2006). Thus, people need to be socialized into a culture of consumption.

While public education became available for blacks following the Civil War, it was consistently underfunded and subpar, and there was minimal effort to enforce the mandatory nature of education for young people (Anderson 1988).

The Pew Forum on Religion & Public Life (2012) garnered a lot of attention when it announced that Protestants were no longer a majority in the United States.

For a history of Catholic Parish schools, see Timothy Walch's book, *Parish School* (Walch 2003). For a history of what it was like to be on the front line in trying to change Bible reading in schools, Madalyn Murray O'Hair's book *An Atheist Epic* (1989) is a fascinating read. For a more historical and scholarly take on those events, there are other options (Dierenfield 2007). Of course, Katherine Stewart's book, *The Good News Club* (2012), is very informative on issues surrounding efforts to reintegrate religion into schools.

There is still a great deal of debate over the origins of Thanksgiving among scholars, but there are a few things we do know: there was no turkey, it didn't take place in 1621, and it wasn't Pilgrims feeding Native Americans (Hodgson 2006). Additionally, while numerous states instituted Thanksgiving holidays before it became a federal holiday, and an annual presidential proclamation made it a holiday every year between 1863 and 1941, it wasn't made a federal holiday until 1941.

While just 16 percent of parents say the primary reason why they home school their kids is to provide religious instruction, 64 percent say it is an important reason (U.S. Department of Education

2012). Additionally, 77 percent report that one of the important reasons why they do so is to provide moral instruction.

Slate recently published an article detailing the spread of charter schools and noting that many of them are teaching creationism (Kirk 2014). Phil Plait (2013) has discussed the use of vouchers to facilitate the teaching of creationism.

There is a lot of research showing that young people tend to have similar religious beliefs, behaviors, and identities to their parents (Acock and Bengtson 1978; Baker-Sperry 2001; Bengtson 2013; Bengtson et al. 2009; Dudley and Dudley 1986; Hayes and Pittelkow 1993; Hoge, Petrillo, and Smith 1982; Hunsberger, Pratt, and Pancer 2001; Myers 1996), though the influence of parents begins to wane as young adults leave home (Arnett and Jensen 2002).

Other researchers have found that college contributes to declines in orthodoxy of religious belief (Funk and Willits 1987; D. C. Johnson 1997), but there isn't necessarily a decline in religious attendance (Lee 2002) or religious identity (Dillon 1996). However, that is largely based on research from the United States. Internationally, it appears as though the single best predictor of declining levels of religiosity is educational attainment (Braun 2012).

Gordon Allport's work on how contact in egalitarian settings can reduce prejudice is still well-regarded (Allport 1979).

Peter Berger (1990) developed the idea that religions provide for their followers a "sacred canopy" or worldview that encompasses the individual and colors how people see the world. That sacred canopy is held up by "plausibility structures," a metaphor for the different aspects of people's lives that help reinforce the plausibility of beliefs —like friends, family, church, clergy, scripture, prayer, ritual, etc.

There is pretty good evidence today to suggest that there are clear benefits to universities and students when a university has a diverse student body (Denson and Chang 2009).

I have provided a detailed explanation of the relationship between science and religion elsewhere (Cragun forthcoming). In short, science and religion can contradict each other, but they don't have to. Really it is fundamentalist religion that most clearly contradicts science (Emerson and Hartman 2006), while liberal religions are typically accepting of science (Cragun 2013a). An excellent illustration of how science has completely undermined fundamentalist beliefs by contradicting literalist interpretations of scripture is the overwhelming body of evidence that contradicts the Noachian flood myth (R. A. Moore 1983).

Perhaps the most famous example of religious fundamentalists taking over state school boards and enacting changes that will contribute to the indoctrination of children is the state of Texas. Since conservative Christians took over that school board, they have tried to remove the word "slavery" from textbooks, replacing it with the phrase "Atlantic triangular trade" (Monroe 2010); this effort failed. But they did succeed in removing Thomas Jefferson from a list of individuals whose writings may have inspired later revolutions, replacing him with the theologian Thomas Aquinas (McKinley Jr. 2010).

My source for the cutting of government funds for education and a shift toward students paying for college is a report from the Washington State Budget and Policy Center (Justice 2011). There is a growing body of research showing that the increase in administrators in colleges and universities has contributed to the increases in tuition rates (Belkin and Thurm 2012). The National Science Foundation has shown that the percentage of the federal budget dedicated to research has declined over time (National Science Foundation 2014). While federal spending on research has declined in the United States, government support for research has been increasing in other countries (Markovich 2012).

For detailed information about Mark Regnerus's very problematic study on children raised by parents who may have had a homosexual encounter at some point in the past, Philip N. Cohen has provided a timeline of events with links to relevant sources on his blog (Cohen 2013). If you'd prefer a slightly less entertaining refutation of Regnerus's flawed study, you can read the American

Sociological Association's Amicus Curiae brief to the Supreme Court instead (Boccuzzi, Jr., Thompson, and Lightner 2013). Information about Mark Regnerus's "institute" can be found here: http://www.austin-institute.org/.

For a detailed discussion of "intelligent design" as a "wedge" strategy to get religion back into public schools, see Forrest and Gross's book, *Creationism's Trojan Horse: The Wedge of Intelligent Design* (2007).

There is pretty good evidence to suggest that the Religious Right helped influence lesbian and gay activism as it developed during the 1960s, 1970s, and 1980s (Fetner 2008).

There is a large body of research showing that getting people to write persuasive essays that will be read by others (i.e., made public) results in the authors of the essays trying to convince themselves of the arguments that they are making (Baumeister 1982; Tice 1992). This is often referred to as cognitive dissonance, but should be understood as a form of impression management—once someone has stated a position publicly, they do not want to seem inconsistent by changing that view at a later point. As a result, they end up actually changing their self-concept and personal views in order to align those views with what they have stated publicly. Is this a little deceptive? Yep. But this is precisely what religions do when they get people to express their beliefs publicly. We're just using the tools of religion against religion.

Step 2: Empower Gender, Sexual, and Racial Minorities
There is plenty of research showing that many religions mistreat women (Chaves 1997; Chalfant, Beckley, and Palmer 1994). Likewise, higher levels of religious fundamentalism have been shown to be related to prejudicial attitudes toward sexual minorities (Cragun and Sumerau forthcoming), and priming people with religious words has been shown to increase racial prejudice (M. K. Johnson, Rowatt, and LaBouff 2010). There is also a long history of religious justification of racial discrimination (Emerson and Smith 2000).

Demographers have long known that more men are born than women, and not just in humans (Grech, Savona-Ventura, and Vassallo-Agius 2002). How disparate the ratio is depends on many factors, including sex selection in utero, leading to very disparate sex ratios in places like India and China. The sex ratio between men and women shifts to about parity in the mid-30s, as men die at younger ages than do women for a variety of reasons (Howden and Meyer 2011).

While there aren't, to date, any comprehensive studies that provide a representative sample of the members of secular groups, there are a few studies that have gathered data on members of these groups using nonrandom samples. In those studies, the majority of secular group members have been white men (Pasquale 2010; Hunsberger 2006). This isn't all that surprising considering the nonreligious and atheists in the United States are disproportionately white and male (Kosmin et al. 2009; Cragun 2014).

A number of studies have found that a chauvinistic culture in male-dominated fields like engineering create a hostile environment for women in those fields, resulting in lower percentages of women wanting to enter those fields (Sappleton and Takruri-Rizk 2008; Logel et al. 2009; Settles et al. 2013).

In the last few years there have been many allegations about sexual harassment at secular conferences (Winston 2012; Watson 2012; Mehta 2013). As far as I am aware, none of those allegations have turned into criminal convictions. I note that there have been no criminal convictions not to suggest that the sexual harassment hasn't occurred but rather to be as fair as possible to those who have been accused of sexual harassment. In part in response to the less than hospitable environment for women in the secular movement, a new organization focused on women has recently come into existence: Secular Woman. For information about this group, see www.secularwoman.org/about. Despite recent attempts to address gender issues in the secular movement, there continue to be issues (Christina 2013; Dearden 2014).

Women do tend to be less prejudiced toward racial and sexual minorities than are men (Cragun and Sumerau forthcoming). The one exception we found in my own research is polygamists; women tend to hold more negative views of polygamists, probably because, as it is typically practiced, it is polygyny, not polyandry or polygamy, and polygyny empowers men and disempowers women.

Many people have written very eloquently about the philosophy of science (Popper 2002; Losee 2001) and science as an avocation (Weber 1946). My concern is with holding up science as the answer to everything, which is commonly referred to as "scientism" (Peterson 2003). In this chapter I noted that there is no such thing as "the view of science." After I wrote that, I realized that *The View of Science* would make a great title for a popular interest magazine.

There is growing evidence that some aspects of human morality are biological (Waal 2014).

A great illustration of science changing as a result of someone questioning the status quo is the idea of plate tectonics. This was a revolutionary idea when it was first introduced but is now the standard model for understanding the earth (Oreskes 2002).

Science was used to oppose masturbation in the past (Stengers and Neck 2001), though science can now be cited to note there are no harms associated with masturbation and that it can contribute to human health (Coleman and Bockting 2003).

While not the only factor contributing to the development of apartheid in South Africa, scientific racism did contribute (Dubow 1995). Science was used to defend slavery in the United States, and later was used to defend segregation as well (Richards 2012). It was also the basis for the eugenics movement in the United States (Black 2012). Conversion therapy for homosexuals was based on science (Drescher, Shidlo, and Schroeder 2002). Intersex individuals have had their genitalia mutilated based on scientific arguments (Fausto-Sterling 2000; Dreger 2000). And, as mentioned, science is currently being used to try to prevent the legalization of same-sex marriage in the United States (Boccuzzi, Jr., Thompson, and Lightner 2013).

There are numerous studies that indicate women continue to do the majority of housework in most homes in the United States (Civettini and Glass 2008; Presser 1994; Hook 2006). The division of housework is even more unequal in religiously conservative homes (Ellison and Bartkowski 2002).

Divorce rates are actually kind of difficult to calculate. It's fairly straightforward to calculate the number of divorces each year, which is usually presented as a rate per 1,000 population. In 2011, that number was 3.6. Marriage rates can be calculated the same way. In 2011, the marriage rate per 1,000 people in the United States was 6.8 (ProQuest Statistical Abstract of the U.S. 2015a). But the estimate that about half of marriages end in divorce is more complicated. There are two ways to calculate this, one of which is much more accurate than the other. First, you can simply divide the divorce rate by the marriage rate. This comes out to close to 50%, but this is deceptive because it's comparing the number of marriages that took place in any given year to the number of divorces that took place in that same year, and that doesn't tell us precisely what percentage of marriages ended, only that about half as many divorces are taking place as marriages. The more precise method of calculating divorce rates is to track marriages over time. That, of course, is much more difficult to do as it requires time, money, and keeping track of specific marriages. In the few studies that have done this, we end up with a similar number—around 50% (Copen et al. 2012). When divorces do occur, women are more likely to get custody of the children, though shared custody has increased pretty dramatically over the last twenty years or so (Cancian et al. 2014). Another trend in family arrangements has been the increasing number of people opting to cohabit rather than marry, and many of those couples end up having kids—particularly outside the United States (Cherlin 2004; Lichter, Turner, and Sassler 2010).

Research looking at the transmission of religion from parents to children has found that kids are more like their mothers than their fathers in their religiosity (Cragun 2013a; Acock and Bengtson

1978). Given the rising rates of nonreligious people in the United States (Kosmin et al. 2009; Chaves 2011), it's not surprising that a growing percentage of children are being raised outside of religions (Merino 2011).

While we don't know precisely what percentage of the U.S. population is lesbian, gay, bisexual, transgender, or queer, estimates suggest somewhere close to 5 percent are lesbian, gay, bisexual, or transgender. Additionally, about 1 in 10 Americans report at least some same-sex sexual attraction and about 8 percent of Americans have engaged in same-sex sexual behavior at some point in their lives (Gates 2011). Increasingly, states are allowing same-sex couples to adopt (Brodzinsky and Pertman 2011), which will contribute to more children being raised by LGBTQ couples.

Hispanics have the highest birth rates in the United States, at 17.6 per 1,000 population. Blacks are second, at 14.7 per 1,000. Whites have the lowest birth rates at 10.8 per 1,000 (ProQuest Statistical Abstract of the U.S. 2015b). The U.S. Census Bureau is estimating that non-Hispanic whites will lose their majority status by 2043 (U.S. Census Bureau Public Information Office 2012).

While nonreligious Americans are less racist than are religious Americans today (Cragun 2013a), that doesn't mean there are no racist nonreligious people. One rather notorious atheist who was racist and anti-Semitic was James Hervey Johnson, the editor of *The Truth Seeker* (Edwords 2007).

While the primary opposition to same-sex marriage in the United States is still based on religion (Cragun and Kosmin 2013), a growing number of religions have changed their policies allowing lesbians and gays to participate at every level of the religion (Kaleem 2014; United Church of Christ 1985) and are even supporting the legalization of same-sex marriage (United Church of Christ 2005). To what extent these changes in policies are specifically so the religions can recruit among sexual and gender minorities versus simply being tolerant and accepting of existing members isn't entirely clear, but it is likely part of the motivation behind the changes.

Single men and women are less likely to be religious (Stolzenberg, Blair-Loy, and Waite 1995), even when age is controlled (Kosmin et al. 2009). Cohabiting has also been shown to reduce religiosity (Thornton, Axinn, and Hill 1992), as I illustrated in this chapter. Women in more conservative religions are less likely to work outside the home, reducing family earnings (Fitzgerald and Glass 2008; Glass and Nath 2006; Glass and Jacobs 2005). Fundamentalist religions do discourage the pursuit of education for both young men and women (Darnell and Sherkat 1997). Religions have actively worked against the rights of women (Chalfant, Beckley, and Palmer 1994)—for instance, among the organized opposition to the Equal Rights Amendment that would have guaranteed greater equality for women was a coalition of religions (Mansbridge 1986; E. E. Gordon and Gillespie 2012; Critchlow and Stachecki 2008).

There is a long history of primarily male doctors prescribing or performing hysterectomies unnecessarily or even without women's consent (Dreifus 1977). Additionally, the medical establishment was initially part of the opposition to birth control in the United States, refusing to prescribe birth control—typically on religious grounds (L. Gordon 2007; McCann 1999).

Women are more likely to identify with and practice a variety of New Age religions, like Wicca (Sered 1994; Sered 1998; Jensen and Thompson 2008; H. A. Berger, Ezzy, and Berger 2009). This is likely the case because such religions are more egalitarian when it comes to gender issues and they provide avenues for female empowerment (Sered 1994).

One of the vexing questions in the social scientific study of religion is why women are more religious than men are in Judeo-Christian religions in the West (Thompson and Remmes 2002; Collett and Lizardo 2009; Miller and Stark 2002); additionally, the gender imbalance is often even more skewed the more conservative the religion (Hoffmann and Bartkowski 2008). One of my favorite explanations is that provided by Linda Woodhead (2008). She suggests that women who—through choice, socialization, biology, or some combinationt thereof—embody more traditional gender roles find greater validation in conservative religions that value such gender roles. While I find this to be one of the more compelling explanations available, in reality we don't have a great explanation for this well-known finding to date.

The paper of mine I cite in this section is called, "The Last Bastion of Sexual and Gender Prejudice? Sexualities, Race, Gender, Religiosity, and Spirituality in the Examination of Prejudice Toward Sexual and Gender Minorities" (Cragun and Sumerau forthcoming). The basic argument of the paper is that religious fundamentalists hold the most negative attitudes toward gender, racial, and sexual minorities, even after controlling for a variety of other variables.

It has only been in the last decade or so that research has compellingly illustrated that people grow more conservative in the face of threats, and this likely has to do with differences in how conservative and progressive individuals think and process information (Jost et al. 2007).

While the motivation to remove Native Americans from their land may have been primarily based on resources, one of the tools used to justify the oppression and assimilation of Native Americans was religion—specifically, the desire to convert Native Americans to Christianity (Talbot 2006). Likewise, part of the justification for the conquering of the rest of the Americas—Central and South America—was rooted in a desire to convert the indigenous populations to Christianity (Taylor 2002). Religion was also used to justify slavery for blacks, even if the primary motivation for slavery was financial (Emerson and Smith 2000). A major component of the modern white supremacist movement, which is rarely mentioned in the media, is conservative Christianity (Aho 1990).

Of course, religion has been helpful in organizing opposition to the oppression of some minorities, as it was instrumental in organizing the Civil Rights Movement (Morris 1984). It should be noted, however, that there were many nonbelievers involved in the movement as well (Pfeffer 1996). Their contributions have largely been downplayed because of a proreligious bias that is pervasive in the United States. A similar proreligious bias has resulted in a diminution of the contributions of nonbelievers in the abolition and women's suffrage movements (Jacoby 2005).

While openly racist views and actions have greatly diminished in the United States, there is still plenty of evidence to support the continued importance of race and the existence of a racialized society. One sociologist coined the phrase "color-blind racism" to refer to this less explicit form of racism that is still pervasive in America (Bonilla-Silva 2010).

Step 3: Provide "This Life" Security

As noted in the notes from the previous chapter, fear and threat anxiety lead people to become more conservative (Jost et al. 2007). There is now research illustrating a link between threats and belief in god, showing that individuals who feel threatened—but also feel like they are powerless to deal with the threat—are more likely to express a belief in a controlling God (Laurin, Kay, and Moscovitch 2008). There is also compelling evidence at a more macro level that insecurity drives desire for religion (Norris and Inglehart 2004). Norris and Inglehart pretty compellingly illustrate that there is a strong relationship between whether a country has a well-developed social safety net (e.g., welfare, retirement benefits, healthcare, unemployment benefits, etc.) and how religious the people are in that country on average. The relationship is inverted—a broader, more well-developed social safety net is strongly correlated with lower levels of religiosity.

Early agriculture was not an exclusive economic system; many early farmers (and many current farmers) supplemented the crops they were growing with other foods they hunted and gathered (Diamond 2005).

Losing one's job can result in a loss of self-esteem and self-efficacy (Anaf et al. 2013). As previously noted, such threats—including a general sense of uncertainty—can lead people to turn toward more conservative political views and to emphasize greater levels of religiosity (Jost et al. 2007; Laurin, Kay, and Moscovitch 2008; Wichman 2010). This is often referred to as the "compensation model" when trying to understand why some people are religious and others are not (Granqvist 1998).

Mark Twain's book, *Captain Stormfield's Visit to Heaven* (2014), is delightfully entertaining and satirical.

Bart Ehrman's book on theodicy, *God's Problem* (2009), clearly elucidates this problem in Christianity. Of course, the problem of evil is a problem for any religion that posits an omnipotent deity that is just.

Phil Zuckerman's insightful research on Danes (Zuckerman 2008) illustrates quite compellingly that, once a certain level of economic development and a robust social safety net are in place, a desire for afterlife security seems to largely disappear.

Data for my analysis in this chapter come from the World Values Survey (World Values Survey 2006).

Losing one's job affects life circumstances in numerous ways: a greater likelihood of homelessness (Murphy, Zemore, and Mulia 2014), higher incidence of alcoholism (Murphy, Zemore, and Mulia 2014), reduction in physical and mental health (Burgard, Brand, and House 2007; Frank, Davis, and Elgar 2014), poorer child development (Kalil 2009), and numerous other problems (Farber 2005).

The alliance between Republicans and the Christian Right is kind of mutually beneficial, but really something of a ploy by Republicans. The Christian Right feel like they have a national voice by influencing the Republican Party, though much of that influence really just results in lip service paid to the socially conservative agenda of the Christian Right by the Republican leadership. Meanwhile, Republicans gain sufficient votes from the alliance with the Christian Right to pursue their fiscally conservative agenda (Williams 2012). There have been specific episodes during this alliance when the leadership of the Republican Party pursued an agenda designed to undermine the advance of secularization, like

Reagan's promise to reverse the successes of the progressive social movements of the 1960s and 1970s in order to push the majority of Americans into economic desperation that would, in turn, result in many Americans turning to religion to find compensation for their shitty mortal life (Duggan 2003). Changes in religiosity over time in the United States show that this strategy actually worked, as religiosity leveled off during the 1980s after some declines in the 1970s (Cragun 2007).

The Tax Foundation has prepared a document of all tax rates from 1862 to 2013 (taxfoundation.org 2013).

While I largely depict religious conservatives and wealthy Republicans being allies but distinct groups, there are those individuals who have their feet firmly planted in both camps—super-wealthy clergy, some of whom make millions of dollars every year (Kaleem 2012; Cragun, Yeager, and Vega 2012).

Step 4—Encourage Sexual Liberation for Everyone
Cognitive dissonance is a social psychological phenomenon that basically suggests people experience anxiety when there is a misalignment between their self-concept and public impressions of them (Baumeister 1982; Aronson 1999). People can hold contradictory beliefs about all sorts of things (e.g., that American football is enjoyable to watch but that brain trauma suffered by football players is wrong), and those contradictory beliefs are unlikely to cause people serious discomfort. However, if someone's conception of who he or she is doesn't align with how other people perceive that individual and that individual is aware of public perceptions, that is when people are likely to experience cognitive dissonance and feel a desire to change one of the two conflicting aspects—either their self-conception or people's perception of them.

The latest data on rates of premarital sex suggest about 95 percent of Americans have sex before marriage (Finer 2007). Attitudes toward premarital sex have grown more accepting over the last thirty years as well (Scott 1998). Cohabitation is also on the rise and attitudes toward cohabitation have changed (Lichter, Turner, and Sassler 2010).

There is a long history of religions trying to regulate sexuality (Posner 1994).

By "cult" I just mean "new religious movement" (which is the preferred term for recently founded religions in the social sciences) and am not speaking pejoratively (Olson 2006; Cragun, Henry, et al. 2012). Of course, in this case, Wayne Bent was an asshole and was seriously creepy (National Geographic Channel 2008). But most cults/new religious movements are far more benign than his was.

While it isn't without its critics, *Sex at Dawn* (Ryan and Jethá 2011) compellingly argues that humans are extremely sexual animals. There are exceptions, as some people are asexual, and interest in sex varies by person. It is important to note, however, that this pattern shows up among asexual people as well. These people often have more developed sexual fantasies and discussions about sex than their more sexual counterparts and often engage in a wide variety of intimate activities, even though our current society, which is often more focused on reproductive-like sex than intimate connection and pleasure, doesn't define them as sexual.

Knowledge about and attitudes toward sex have changed pretty dramatically over time, which is something few people other than sex, gender, and family historians seem to know (Coontz 1992; Posner 1994; Elliott 2012). There is pretty good evidence to suggest that Americans' repressive attitudes toward sex end up harming our sex lives, particularly compared with the more open attitudes toward sex in other developed countries (Elliott 2012).

While my primary research interest is religion, I also teach a college course on the sociology of human sexuality and do a lot of research on religion and sexuality. I also happen to know a few people who would be really good for an evening discussion on sex. In other words, if your group needs some suggestions for people who would be good for a frank discussion about sex and sexuality, feel free to contact me.

There is compelling evidence that abstinence-only sex education does not work in that it doesn't prevent young people from having sex, from getting pregnant, or from contracting sexually transmitted infections and that it may actually increase their risk compared to comprehensive sex education (Santelli et al. 2006; Rosenbaum 2009).

Step 5: Stop Subsidizing Religion and Deregulate It
According to the International Religious Freedom Report, regular religious service attendance in Denmark is around 3 percent (U.S. Department of State 2009) and the European Social Survey indicates only about 2 percent of Norwegians attend religious services on a weekly basis (newsinenglish.no 2009). Attendance is very low despite around 70 percent of people in each country reporting an affiliation with a religion. As is the case in the United Kingdom, being a member of the state church or claiming religious membership is part of the culture in these countries (Day 2013), but membership in a religion indicates virtually nothing about the beliefs or behaviors of Danes or Norwegians.

Both the state churches and the governments in Norway and Denmark have been attempting to increase the separation between the two, allowing the religions greater autonomy (Iverson 2014).

There are many histories of the witch hunts (Levack 2006) and the Spanish Inquisition (Pérez 2006), both of which were horrific, brutal, and largely inspired by religion (Pinker 2012). Persecution of minorities in the name of religion continues today, particularly in predominantly Muslim countries where the execution of LGBTQ individuals is legal (Michaelson 2014), though of course there is still plenty of discrimination against minority groups in other countries as well, much of it motivated by religion (Disha, Cavendish, and King 2011; Cragun, Kosmin, et al. 2012; Hammer et al. 2012; Cragun and Sumerau forthcoming).

While I generally disagree with Rodney Stark's theories regarding religion (Stark and Finke 2000), his point about the pastors of many of the state churches in Europe being less motivated because they do not need to bring in their own salaries is a reasonably good one that has been supported by other research as well (Zuckerman 2008).

The industrial revolution and early capitalism were not kind to the proletariat (Green 2010).

Of the many religions that have been founded over the years, few have drawn as much attention as the Peoples Temple, founded by Jim Jones. Obviously a large part of that is the mass suicide that largely ended the religion, but most people are unaware of the many other nefarious activities of Jones, like him sexual assaulting his followers, regardless of gender or sexual orientation (Scheeres 2012; Layton 1999).

While many secular activists and organizations worry about politicking over the pulpit, there is reason to believe that overt politicking by religious leaders in religious settings may actually be helping the secular movement (Putnam and Campbell 2012). When clergy discuss political issues over the pulpit, members of the religion don't like it and are more likely to leave that congregation. So, really, rather than fighting politicking over the pulpit, secular activists should be encouraging it!

My article in *Free Inquiry* (Cragun, Yeager, and Vega 2012) about the cost of tax donations to the American public is available on my professional Web site: www.ryantcragun.com. Not a lot has been written about the origins of tax exemptions for religions, though there is some research on this (Livingston 2008). There is also evidence from economics that, when donations to religions are tax deductible, people donate more to religions (Randolph 1995).

The Government Accountability Office admitted in 2006 that there is very lackadaisical oversight of faith-based initiatives, and that greater oversight of these programs could help their effectiveness (Government Accountability Office 2006). Others have noted similar problems with these initiatives (Kuo 2007; Sager 2009).

While my article estimating the subsidy from government to religions through tax exemptions received a lot of attention (Cragun, Yeager, and Vega 2012), it is worth noting that it is a problematic article for a variety of reasons. The biggest problem with the article is really due to a misunderstanding. Some people failed to realize that the article was always intended to be a thought experiment and not a precise estimate of tax revenue loss through privileging of religions (in part because I'm not an accountant or tax lawyer). My coauthors and I thought we had made this clear in the article when we noted that, for the purposes of the paper, we were going to treat religions as though they were the equivalent of movie theaters or some other for-profit corporation. Anyone familiar with tax policy would immediately recognize the problematic nature of such a comparison, which we readily admitted. But, in a thought experiment, such assumptions are allowed. In reality, while I disagree with the tax exemptions for religions, I think a more accurate way of estimating the cost of such subsidies would be to treat religions as something more akin to Freemasons or other fraternal societies, organizations that still benefit from numerous tax exemptions. These organizations receive special tax treatment from the IRS, but their exemption rests upon the belief that a fraternal order is beneficial to society, which is a more compelling argument than religion being beneficial to society. I'd settle for all religions switching to fraternal society exemptions so long as they are held to the same criteria as fraternal societies are.

Step 6: Encourage Regulated Capitalism
There are many articles and books that have used the metaphor of a "religious marketplace" to try to understand religions in pluralistic societies (Kosmin and Keysar 2006; B. Martin 2006; R. L. Moore 1995; Cragun and Nielsen 2009).

While precise numbers are unknown, the Catholic Church has likely paid out billions in settlement fees resulting from the various abuse cases it has settled (Cozzens 2000). A number of these settlements have resulted in dioceses filing for bankruptcy protection (Urbina 2009; Clark 2006).

According to the U.S. Census Bureau, 1.5 percent of Americans had professional degrees and another 1.7 percent of Americans had doctoral degrees in 2013 (U.S. Census Bureau 2013).

I only know about tabloids because I do the grocery shopping and can't help but look at all the photoshopped pictures of aliens and celebrities, and celebrity aliens, and alien-like celebrities. I can also proudly say I've never actually watched an episode of *Entertainment Tonight* of my own accord. Some of my family members used to watch it, so I know it exists, and I may have been in the same room when it was on, but I've never actually sat through an episode.

Americans have some knowledge about science (Pew Research Center 2013), but the percentages who get obvious things wrong can be rather disturbing. For instance, 48 percent of Americans think lasers work by focusing sound waves, and just 20 percent know that nitrogen makes up most of the atmosphere.

My source for the percentage of Americans who are intellectually curious (~40%) is a little problematic as it is based on a marketing study conducted by a research firm that was trying to gauge how many Americans would be interested in consuming science-related news (Britt 2006). A hard cutoff for the percentage who are intellectually curious is probably an oversimplification of this phenomenon, considering curiosity is really measured along a continuum (Litman and Spielberger 2003).

I make a killer zucchini bread. E-mail me for the recipe.

Typical surveys on religious attendance suggest about 40 percent of Americans report attending religious services on a weekly basis, but closer scrutiny of those numbers has found that the actual percentage is about half of that, or 20 percent of Americans (Hadaway, Marler, and Chaves 1993).

My source for the amount of money donated to religions every year in the United States is the Giving USA annual report, which can be found here: http://givingusareports.org/.

The St. Paul Saints have made it something of a tradition to change their name once a year both to honor the Minnesota Atheists, who sponsor their game that night, and to help raise funds for the charitable efforts of the Minnesota Atheists (Rupar 2013).

Step 7: Support Education, Art, and Science
These people are basically the inverse of the group discussed in Step 6—those who are intellectually curious (Litman and Spielberger 2003; Britt 2006).

Step 8: Syncretize Holidays and Rituals
While there is some debate among secular individuals as to which holidays to celebrate, how to celebrate them, and the importance of rituals, I think most secular individuals generally agree that holidays are a good thing. The concern is over their religious connotations. For instance, Tom Flynn, the editor of *Free Inquiry*, doesn't celebrate Christmas (Flynn 1992), while many other secular individuals do (Harvie and Meyers 2010). The American Humanist Society, an adjunct of the American Humanist Association, recognizing the desire of many secular individuals for rituals, has developed a training and certification program for humanist celebrants to assist with rituals: http://humanist-society.org/.

I'm consistently surprised by how few people are familiar with the idea of syncretism (Leopold and Jensen 2004). The only way to really understand religion is to also understand syncretism (Witzel 2013). For instance, the celebration of saints in Latin America is a manifestation of Catholic syncretism (Watanabe 1990; Nutini 1976; Camara 1988). Of course, the introduction of saints into Christianity goes much further back into the history of the religion, as does the syncretism of Christmas, Easter, and Halloween (Bede 1991; Walter and Lecouteux 2014).

A very readable introduction to the origins of Islam is Reza Aslan's book, *No god but God* (Aslan 2011). Likewise, Robert Goldenberg's book, *The Origins of Judaism*, is also a good primer on the subject (Goldenberg 2013).

While I do think Santa Claus is more benign than the Jewish/Muslim/Christian monotheistic God, I don't love Santa Claus. Parents who opt to teach their kids to believe in Santa Claus should: (1) not teach them that Santa is always watching (Cragun 2013b), and (2) realize that they are increasing the odds that their children will have a hard time distinguishing between fantasy and reality (Corriveau, Chen, and Harris 2014).

President Barack Obama has hosted *iftar* (the nightly meal that breaks a day's fast during Ramadan) at the White House, as have other presidents, like Bill Clinton and George W. Bush (Associated Press 2012).

My references to Jesus being a Jewish zealot come from another book by Reza Aslan, *Zealot* (2014).

While I provided references on the origins of Thanksgiving earlier, it is also worth noting that there is a growing body of research suggesting that giving thanks and showing gratitude are beneficial to both physical and mental health. This is especially true for mental health (Emmons and Stern 2013; Hill, Allemand, and Roberts 2013; Krause and Hayward 2014; Krause et al. 2014; Sandage, Hill, and Vaubel 2011).

Using what I think are fairly objective criteria—living longer, healthier, and less violent lives—there is pretty compelling evidence that humans have seen substantial improvements over time (Diamond 2005; Pinker 2012).

Research on vacations from work do indicate a pretty quick and substantial improvement in health and well-being. However, the effect is relatively short-lived for most people—after just a week or two back at work, the benefits to health and well-being have largely dissipated (Bloom, Geurts, and Kompier 2013; de Bloom et al. 2011; de Bloom et al. 2010). There is compelling research suggesting mostly mental health benefits from spending time in nature and outdoors (Berman, Jonides, and Kaplan 2008; Song et al. 2013), particularly in active pursuits, but not as much evidence that exercising outside is better for your physical health than exercising inside (Thompson Coon et al. 2011). Singing offers a number of health benefits, including better breathing, but also, if done as part of a group or choir, a greater sense of belonging and camaraderie (Gick 2011). Systematic reviews of the literature on meditation suggest reductions in psychological stress resulting from meditation (Goyal et al. 2014).

Step 9: Change Society to Value Critical Thinking and Scientific Inquiry

There is a lot of evidence indicating that being religious is normative in the United States (Edgell, Gerteis, and Hartmann 2006; Cragun, Kosmin, et al. 2012). Recent research has established that much of the dislike and antipathy toward atheists in the United States is based on trust. Theists have a hard time trusting atheists because they don't think atheists are trustworthy without a god watching them (Gervais, Shariff, and Norenzayan 2011; Gervais 2011; Norenzayan 2013).

The survey I'm referring to in Europe in which religion was ranked last is the Eurobarometer 69 (European Commission 2008).

If you don't know how George Takei says "Oh my!" go here now: http://youtu.be/6nSKkwzwdW4

Humanism has been recognized as a religion by the courts several times, most recently as relates to religions prison inmates can adhere to (Ashtari 2014).

Step 10: Teach Humanist Ethics in School

Forrest and Gross (2007) provide an excellent discussion of creationism's "wedge" strategy.

In one of my research projects we found that religious fundamentalists can learn about evolution, and that they do at about the same rate as do nonfundamentalists (Cragun, Cragun, and Creighton 2012). However, they started out with less knowledge. We didn't follow up long term to see how much knowledge they retained after we taught them about evolution, but after about six weeks, religious fundamentalists had retained some knowledge about evolution. We interpreted our results to suggest that religious fundamentalists likely compartmentalize different aspects of their lives such that what they learn about evolution does not influence what they believe about the origins of humans from their religion.

Will Gervais, a psychologist at the University of Kentucky,

has probably done more than any other scholar to understand why atheists are so disliked in the United States. His research has consistently shown that the dislike of atheists is rooted in trust—a significant proportion of Americans distrust atheists (Gervais, Shariff, and Norenzayan 2011; Gervais and Norenzayan 2012). There is also a lot of research showing that stereotypes of atheists are rooted in a sense of atheists' immorality (Heiner 1992; Jenks 1986; Harper 2007; Bloesch, Forbes, and Adams-Curtis 2004).

I found the Vice.com (Saward 2014) article particularly disturbing because it reminds me of so many of my students. I mentioned the article to some of my sociology colleagues and one suggested that this behavior, while deplorable, is fully expected within the theoretical reasoning of recent research suggesting that men are increasingly engaged in "manhood acts"—actions that allow these individuals to create their gender (a hypermasculine gender) and, in the process, attempt to subordinate other genders (Schrock and Schwalbe 2009).

Conclusion

I've mentioned secularization several times in the book. The basic idea is that religiosity declines as a result of modernization. The decline of religiosity can be manifested in many ways—people leaving religion, people ignoring the dictates of their religion, people criticizing religion, a declining sense of trust or respect for religion, a weakening of influence of religion over other aspects of society, etc. For a clear explanation of secularization, the best book at the moment is Steve Bruce's latest, *Secularization: In Defence of an Unfashionable Theory* (2013).

BIBLIOGRAPHY

Acock, Alan C., and Vern L. Bengtson. 1978. "On the Relative Influence of Mothers and Fathers: A Covariance Analysis of Political and Religious Socialization." *Journal of Marriage and the Family* 40 (3): 519–30.

Aho, James Alfred. 1990. *The Politics of Righteousness: Idaho Christian Patriotism*. Washington: University of Washington Press.

Allport, Gordon W. 1979. *The Nature Of Prejudice: 25th Anniversary Edition*. Unabridged. Basic Books.

Anaf, Julia, Frances Baum, Lareen Newman, Anna Ziersch, and Gwyneth Jolley. 2013. "The Interplay between Structure and Agency in Shaping the Mental Health Consequences of Job Loss." *BMC Public Health* 13 (1): 1–12. doi:10.1186/1471-2458-13-110.

Anderson, James D. 1988. *The Education of Blacks in the South, 1860-1935*. 1 edition. Chapel Hill: The University of North Carolina Press.

Antoun, Richard T. 2008. *Understanding Fundamentalism: Christian, Islamic, and Jewish Movements*. Second Edition. Rowman & Littlefield Publishers.

Arnett, Jeffrey Jensen, and Lene Arnett Jensen. 2002. "A Congregation of One: Individualized Religious Beliefs Among Emerging Adults." *Journal of Adolescent Research* 17 (5): 451–67.

Aronson, Elliot. 1999. "Dissonance, Hypocrisy, and the Self-Concept." In *Readings About the Social Animal*. Worth Publishers.

Ashtari, Shadee. 2014. "Federal Court Ruling Extends Equal Protection Rights To Atheists." *Huffington Post*. November 3. http://www.huffingtonpost.com/2014/11/03/atheist-religion-oregon-court_n_6095776.html.

Aslan, Reza. 2011. *No god but God (Updated Edition): The Origins, Evolution, and Future of Islam*. Updated edition. New York: Random House Trade Paperbacks.

———. 2014. *Zealot: The Life and Times of Jesus of Nazareth*. Reprint edition. Random House Trade Paperbacks.

Bade, Mary K., and Stephen W. Cook. 2008. "Functions of Christian Prayer in the Coping Process." *Journal for the Scientific Study of Religion* 47 (1): 123–33. doi:doi:10.1111/j.1468-5906.2008.00396.x.

Baker-Sperry, Lori. 2001. "Passing on the Faith: The Father's Role in Religious Transmission." *Sociological Focus* 34 (2): 185–98.

Baumeister, Roy F. 1982. "A Self-Presentational View of Social Phenomena." *Psychological Bulletin* 91 (1): 3–26. doi:http://dx.doi.org/10.1037/0033-2909.91.1.3.

Bede. 1991. *Ecclesiastical History of the English People*. Edited by D. H. Farmer and Ronald Latham. Translated by Leo Sherley-Price. Revised edition. New York: Penguin Classics.

Belkin, Douglas, and Scott Thurm. 2012. "Deans List: Hiring Spree Fattens College Bureaucracy—And Tuition." *The Wall Street Journal*, December 28. http://www.wsj.com/articles/SB10001424127887323316804578161490716042814.

Bendix, Reinhard. 1978. *Max Weber: An Intellectual Portrait*. University of California Press.

Bengtson, Vern L. 2013. *Families and Faith: How Religion Is Passed down across Generations*. New York: Oxford University Press.

Bengtson, Vern L., Casey E. Copen, Norella M. Putney, and Merril Silverstein. 2009. "A Longitudinal Study of the Intergenerational Transmission of Religion." *International Sociology* 24 (3): 325–45. doi:10.1177/0268580909102911.

Berger, Helen A, Douglas Ezzy, and Helen A. Berger. 2009. "Mass Media and Religious Identity: A Case Study of Young Witches." *Journal for the Scientific Study of Religion* 48 (3): 501–14.

Berger, Peter L. 1990. *The Sacred Canopy: Elements of a Sociological Theory of Religion*. Anchor.

Berger, Peter L., and Thomas Luckmann. 1967. *The Social Construction of Reality: A Treatise in the Sociology of Knowledge*. Anchor.

Berman, Marc G., John Jonides, and Stephen Kaplan. 2008. "The Cognitive Benefits of Interacting With Nature." *Psychological Science* 19 (12): 1207–12. doi:10.1111/j.1467-9280.2008.02225.x.

Black, Edwin. 2012. *War Against the Weak: Eugenics and America's Campaign to Create a Master Race, Expanded Edition*. Expanded edition. Washington, DC: Dialog Press.

Bloesch, Emily, Gordon B Forbes, and Leah E Adams-Curtis. 2004. "A Brief, Reliable Measure of Negative Attitudes toward Atheists." *Psychological Reports* 95 (3 Pt 2): 1161–62.

Bloom, Jessica, Sabine Geurts, and Michiel Kompier. 2013. "Vacation (after-) Effects on Employee Health and Well-Being, and the Role of Vacation Activities, Experiences and Sleep." *Journal of Happiness Studies* 14 (2): 613–33. doi:10.1007/s10902-012-9345-3.

Boccuzzi, Jr., Carmine D., Scott Thompson, and Mark Lightner. 2013. "Brief of Amicus Curiae American Sociological Association in Support of Respondent Kristin M. Perry and Respondent Edith Schlain Windsor." American Sociological Association. http://www. asanet.org/documents/ASA/pdfs/12-144_307_Amicus_%20 %28C_%20Gottlieb%29_ASA_Same-Sex_Marriage.pdf.

Bonilla-Silva, Eduardo. 2010. *Racism without Racists: Color-Blind Racism and the Persistence of Racial Inequality in the United States*. Lanham: Rowman & Littlefield Publishers.

Braun, Claude M. J. 2012. "Explaining Global Secularity: Existential Security or Education?" *Secularism and Nonreligion* 1 (November). doi:10.5334/snr.ae.

Britt, Robert Roy. 2006. "Beyond the Geeks: 60 Million Americans Labeled 'Intellectually Curious.'" *LiveScience.com*. April 19. http://www.livescience.com/4088-geeks-60-million-americans-labeled-intellectually-curious.html.

Brodzinsky, David M., and Adam Pertman, eds. 2011. *Adoption by Lesbians and Gay Men: A New Dimension in Family Diversity*. New York: Oxford University Press.

Bruce, Steve. 2002. *God Is Dead: Secularization in the West*. London: Blackwell Publishers.

———. 2013. *Secularization: In Defence of an Unfashionable Theory*. Oxford: Oxford University Press.

Burgard, Sarah A., Jennie E. Brand, and James S. House. 2007. "Toward a Better Estimation of the Effect of Job Loss on Health." *Journal of Health & Social Behavior* 48 (4): 369–84.

Cady, Daniel. 2010. "Freethinkers and Hell Raisers: The Brief History of American Atheism and Secularism." In *Atheism and Secularity: Volume 1 - Issues, Concepts, and Definitions*, edited by Phil Zuckerman, 1:229–50. Santa Barbara, CA: Praeger.

Camara, Evandro M. 1988. "Afro-American Religious Syncretism in Brazil and the United States: A Weberian Perspective." *Sociological Analysis* 48 (4): 299. doi:10.2307/3710869.

Cancian, Maria, Daniel R. Meyer, Patricia R. Brown, and Steven T. Cook. 2014. "Who Gets Custody Now? Dramatic Changes in Children's Living Arrangements After Divorce." *Demography* 51 (4): 1381–96. doi:10.1007/s13524-014-0307-8.

Chalfant, H. Paul, Robert E. Beckley, and C. Eddie Palmer. 1994. "Religion, Women, and Religious Organizations." In *Religion in Contemporary Society*, edited by H. Paul Chalfant, Robert E. Beckley, and C. Eddie Palmer, 3rd:403–25. Peacock Publishers.

Chaves, Mark. 1997. *Ordaining Women: Culture and Conflict in Religious Organizations*. Cambridge: Harvard University Press.

———. 2011. *American Religion: Contemporary Trends*. Princeton University Press.

Cherlin, Andrew J. 2004. "The Deinstitutionalization of American Marriage." *Journal of Marriage & Family* 66 (4): 848–61.

Christina, Greta. 2013. "He Treated Us With Contempt: The Context of Ron Lindsay's WiS2 Talk." *Greta Christina's Blog*. May 30. http://freethoughtblogs.com/greta/2013/05/30/contempt-ron-lindsay-context/.

Civettini, Nicole H. W., and Jennifer Glass. 2008. "The Impact of Religious Conservativism on Men's Work and Family Involvement." *Gender & Society* 22 (2): 172–93.

Clark, Amy. 2006. "Iowa Diocese Files For Bankruptcy." News. *CBS News*. October 10. http://www.cbsnews.com/news/iowa-diocese-files-for-bankruptcy/.

Cliteur, P. B. 2010. *The Secular Outlook: In Defense of Moral and Political Secularism*. Chichester, West Sussex: Wiley-Blackwell.

Cohen, Philip N. 2013. "Regnerus Affair Timeline, with Maze." Blog. *Family Inequality*. August 6. https://familyinequality.wordpress.com/2013/08/06/regnerus-affair-timeline-with-maze/.

Coleman, Edmond J., and Walter O. Bockting. 2003. *Masturbation as a Means of Achieving Sexual Health*. New York: Routledge.

Collett, Jessica L., and Omar Lizardo. 2009. "A Power-Control Theory of Gender and Religiosity." *Journal for the Scientific Study of Religion* 48 (2): 213–31.

Coontz, Stephanie. 1992. *The Way We Never Were: American Families and the Nostalgia Trap*. New York, NY: BasicBooks.

Copen, Casey E., Kimberly Daniels, Jonathan Vespa, and W. D. Mosher. 2012. *First Marriages in the United States: Data From the 2006-2010 National Survey of Family Growth*. 49. National Health Statistics Reports. Atlanta, GA: U.S. Department of Health and Human Services. http://www.cdc.gov/nchs/data/nhsr/nhsr049.pdf.

Corriveau, Kathleen H., Eva E. Chen, and Paul L. Harris. 2014. "Judgments About Fact and Fiction by Children From Religious and Nonreligious Backgrounds." *Cognitive Science*, doi:10.1111/cogs.12138.

Cozzens, Donald B. 2000. *The Changing Face of the Priesthood: A Reflection on the Priest's Crisis of Soul*. Collegeville, Minn: Liturgical Press.

Cragun, Ryan T. (forthcoming). "Science and Religion." *International Encyclopedia of Social and Behavioral Sciences*. Oxford, UK: Elsevier.

———. 2007. "A Role Conflict Theory of Religious Change: An Explanation and Test." Dissertation, Cincinnati, OH: University of Cincinnati.

———. 2013a. *What You Don't Know About Religion (but Should)*. Durham, NC: Pitchstone Publishing.

———. 2013b. "On the 'Evils' of Santa Claus." *Free Inquiry*.

———. 2014. "Who Are the 'New Atheists'?." In *Atheist Identities: Spaces and Social Contexts*, edited by Steven Tomlins and Lori Beamon. Springer.

Cragun, Ryan T., Deborah L. Cragun, and Jason Creighton. 2012. "The Influence of Fundamentalist Beliefs on Evolution Knowledge Retention." In *Religion and Knowledge*, edited by Matthew Guest and Elisabeth Arweck, 199–226. London, UK: Ashgate.

Cragun, Ryan T., Patrick Henry, Casey P. Homan, and Joseph H. Hammer. 2012. "Whom Do People Dislike More: Atheists or Cultists?" *Interdisciplinary Journal of Research on Religion* 8: 1–19.

Cragun, Ryan T., and Barry A. Kosmin. 2013. "Cheating or Leveling the Playing Field? Rethinking How We Ask Questions About Religion in the United States." *Free Inquiry*.

Cragun, Ryan T., Barry A. Kosmin, Ariela Keysar, Joseph H. Hammer, and Michael E. Nielsen. 2012. "On the Receiving End: Discrimination Toward the Non-Religious." *Journal of Contemporary Religion* 27 (1): 105–27.

Cragun, Ryan T., and Michael Nielsen. 2009. "Fighting Over 'Mormon': Media Coverage of the FLDS and LDS." *Dialogue: A Journal of Mormon Thought* 43 (4): 65–104.

Cragun, Ryan T., and J. Edward Sumerau. forthcoming. "The Last Bastion of Sexual and Gender Prejudice? Sexualities, Race, Gender, Religiosity, and Spirituality in the Examination of Prejudice Toward Sexual and Gender Minorities." *Journal of Sex Research*, doi:10.1080/00224499.2014.925534.

Cragun, Ryan T., Stephanie Yeager, and Desmond Vega. 2012. "Research Report: How Secular Humanists (and Everyone Else) Subsidize Religion in the United States." *Free Inquiry*.

Critchlow, Donald T., and Cynthia L. Stachecki. 2008. "The Equal Rights Amendment Reconsidered: Politics, Policy, and Social Mobilization in a Democracy." *Journal of Policy History* 20 (1): 157–76.

Darnell, A., and D. E. Sherkat. 1997. "The Impact of Protestant Fundamentalism on Educational Attainment." *American Sociological Review* 62 (2): 306–15.

Day, Abby. 2013. *Believing in Belonging: Belief and Social Identity in the Modern World*. Reprint edition. Oxford University Press.

Dearden, Lizzie. 2014. "Richard Dawkins Tweets: 'Date Rape Is Bad, Stranger Rape Is Worse.'" *The Independent*. July 29. http://www.independent.co.uk/news/people/richard-dawkins-says-date-rape-is-bad-stranger-rape-is-worse-on-twitter-9634572.html.

De Bloom, Jessica, Sabine A.E. Geurts, Sabine Sonnentag, Toon Taris, Carolina de Weerth, and Michiel A.J. Kompier. 2011. "How Does a Vacation from Work Affect Employee Health and Well-Being?" *Psychology & Health* 26 (12): 1606–22. doi:10.1080/08870446.2010.546860.

De Bloom, Jessica, Sabine A. E. Geurts, Toon W. Taris, Sabine Sonnentag, Carolina de Weerth, and Michiel A. J. Kompier. 2010. "Effects of Vacation from Work on Health and Well-Being: Lots of Fun, Quickly Gone." *Work & Stress* 24 (2): 196–216. doi: 10.1080/02678373.2010.493385.

Denson, Nida, and Mitchell J. Chang. 2009. "Racial Diversity Matters: The Impact of Diversity-Related Student Engagement and Institutional Context." *American Educational Research Journal* 46 (2): 322–53.

Diamond, Jared M. 2005. *Guns, Germs, and Steel: The Fates of Human Societies*. New York: Norton.

Dierenfield, Bruce J. 2007. *The Battle over School Prayer: How Engel v. Vitale Changed America*. Lawrence, KS: University Press of Kansas.

Dillon, Michele. 1996. "The Persistence of Religious Identity Among College Catholics." *Journal for the Scientific Study of Religion* 35 (2): 165.

Disha, Ilir, James C. Cavendish, and Ryan D. King. 2011. "Historical Events and Spaces of Hate: Hate Crimes Against Arabs and Muslims in Post 9/11 America." *Social Problems* 58 (1): 21–46.

Dreger, Alice Domurat. 2000. *Hermaphrodites and the Medical Invention of Sex*. Cambridge, Mass.: Harvard University Press.

Dreifus, Claudia. 1977. *Seizing Our Bodies*. 1st edition. New York: Vintage.

Drescher, Jack, Ariel Shidlo, and Michael Schroeder. 2002. *Sexual Conversion Therapy: Ethical, Clinical, and Research Perspectives*. New York: CRC Press.

Dubow, Saul. 1995. *Scientific Racism in Modern South Africa*. Cambridge: Cambridge University Press.

Dudley, Roger L., and Margaret G. Dudley. 1986. "Transmission of Religious Values from Parents to Adolescents." *Review of Religious Research* 28 (1): 3–15.

Duggan, Lisa. 2003. *The Twilight of Equality?: Neoliberalism, Cultural Politics, and the Attack on Democracy*. Boston: Beacon Press.

Durkheim, Emile. 1995. *The Elementary Forms of Religious Life*. Free Press.

Edgell, Penny, Joseph Gerteis, and Douglas Hartmann. 2006. "Atheists As 'Other': Moral Boundaries and Cultural Membership in American Society." *American Sociological Review* 71: 211–34.

Edwords, Fred. 2007. "Johnson, James Hervey." In *The New Encyclopedia of Unbelief*, edited by Tom Flynn, 451–52. Amherst, N.Y.: Prometheus Books.

Ehrman, Bart D. 2009. *God's Problem: How the Bible Fails to Answer Our Most Important Question--Why We Suffer*. Reprint edition. New York: HarperOne.

Eller, David. 2010. "The Cultures of Christianities." In *The Christian Delusion: Why Faith Fails*, edited by John W Loftus, 25–46. Amherst, N.Y.: Prometheus Books.

Elliott, Sinikka. 2012. *Not My Kid: What Parents Believe about the Sex Lives of Their Teenagers*. New York: NYU Press.

Ellison, Christopher G., and John P. Bartkowski. 2002. "Conservative Protestantism and the Division of Household Labor Among Married Couples." *Journal of Family Issues* 23 (8): 950–85.

Emerson, Michael O., and David Hartman. 2006. "The Rise of Religious Fundamentalism." *Annual Review of Sociology* 32 (1): 127–44.

Emerson, Michael O., and Christian Smith. 2000. *Divided by Faith: Evangelical Religion and the Problem of Race in America*. New York: Oxford University Press.

Emmons, Robert A., and Robin Stern. 2013. "Gratitude as a Psychotherapeutic Intervention." *Journal of Clinical Psychology* 69 (8): 846–55. doi:10.1002/jclp.22020.

European Commission. 2008. *Eurobarometer 69: Values of Europeans*. Eurobaromter. http://ec.europa.eu/public_opinion/archives/eb/eb69/eb69_values_en.pdf.

Farber, Henry S. 2005. "What Do We Know about Job Loss in the United States? Evidence from the Displaced Workers Survey, 1984–2004." *Economic Perspectives* 29 (2): 13–28.

Fausto-Sterling, Anne. 2000. *Sexing the Body: Gender Politics and the Construction of Sexuality*. New Ed edition. New York, NY: Basic Books.

Fetner, Tina. 2008. *How the Religious Right Shaped Lesbian and Gay Activism*. Minneapolis: University of Minnesota Press. http://public.eblib.com/EBLPublic/PublicView.do?ptiID=433178.

Finer, Lawrence B. 2007. "Trends in Premarital Sex in the United States, 1954–2003." *Public Health Reports* 122 (1): 73.

Fitzgerald, Scott T., and Jennifer Glass. 2008. "Can Early Family Formation Explain the Lower Educational Attainment of U.S. Conservative Protestants?" *Sociological Spectrum* 28 (5): 556–77.

Flynn, Tom. 1992. *The Trouble with Christmas*. Buffalo, N.Y: Prometheus Books.

Forrest, Barbara, and Paul R. Gross. 2007. *Creationism's Trojan Horse: The Wedge of Intelligent Design*. Oxford University Press, USA.

Frank, Christine, Christopher G. Davis, and Frank J. Elgar. 2014. "Financial Strain, Social Capital, and Perceived Health during Economic Recession: A Longitudinal Survey in Rural Canada." *Anxiety, Stress & Coping* 27 (4): 422–38. doi:10.1080/10615806.2013.864389.

Funk, R. B., and F. K. Willits. 1987. "College Attendance and Attitude-Change: A Panel Study, 1970-81." *Sociology of Education* 60 (4): 224–31.

Gates, Gary J. 2011. *How Many People Are Lesbian, Gay, Bisexual and Transgender?*. The Williams Institute. http://williamsinstitute.law.ucla.edu/wp-content/uploads/Gates-How-Many-People-LGBT-Apr-2011.pdf.

Gervais, Will M. 2011. "Finding the Faithless: Perceived Atheist Prevalence Reduces Anti-Atheist Prejudice." *Personality and Social Psychology Bulletin* 37 (4): 543–56. doi:10.1177/0146167211399583.

Gervais, Will M, and Ara Norenzayan. 2012. "Reminders of Secular Authority Reduce Believers' Distrust of Atheists." *Psychological Science*, 23 (5): 483–491. doi:10.1177/0956797611429711.

Gervais, Will M., Azim F. Shariff, and Ara Norenzayan. 2011. "Do You Believe in Atheists? Distrust Is Central to Anti-Atheist Prejudice." *Journal of Personality and Social Psychology* 101 (6): 1189–1206.

Gick, Mary L. 2011. "Singing, Health and Well-Being: A Health Psychologist's Review." *Psychomusicology: Music, Mind & Brain* 21 (1/2): 176–207. doi:10.1037/h0094011.

Glass, Jennifer, and Jerry Jacobs. 2005. "Childhood Religious Conservatism and Adult Attainment among Black and White Women." *Social Forces* 84 (1): 551–73.

Glass, Jennifer, and Leda E. Nath. 2006. "Religious Conservatism and Women's Market Behavior Following Marriage and Childbirth." *Journal of Marriage & Family* 68 (3): 611–29.

Goldenberg, Robert. 2013. *The Origins of Judaism: From Canaan to the Rise of Islam*. New York: Cambridge University Press.

Gordon, Elizabeth Ellen, and William L. Gillespie. 2012. "The Culture of Obedience and the Politics of Stealth: Mormon Mobilization Against ERA and Same-Sex Marriage." *Politics and Religion* 5 (02): 343–66. doi:10.1017/S1755048312000065.

Gordon, Linda. 2007. *The Moral Property of Women: A History of Birth Control Politics in America*. Urbana: University of Illinois Press.

Government Accountability Office. 2006. *Faith-Based and Community Initiative: Improvements in Monitoring Grantees and Measuring Performance Could Enhance Accountability*. Report to Congressional Requesters GAO-06-616. Washington D.C.: Government Accountability Office. http://www.gao.gov/new.items/d06616.pdf.

Goyal, Madhav, Sonal Singh, Erica M. S. Sibinga, Neda F. Gould, Anastasia Rowland-Seymour, Ritu Sharma, Zackary Berger, et al. 2014. "Meditation Programs for Psychological Stress and Well-Being: A Systematic Review and Meta-Analysis." *JAMA Internal Medicine* 174 (3): 357–68. doi:10.1001/jamainternmed.2013.13018.

Granqvist, Pehr. 1998. "Religiousness and Perceived Childhood Attachment: On the Question of Compensation or Correspondence." *Journal for the Scientific Study of Religion* 37 (2): 350–67.

Grech, Victor, Charles Savona-Ventura, and P. Vassallo-Agius. 2002. "Unexplained Differences in Sex Ratios at Birth in Europe and North America." *BMJ* 324 (7344): 1010–11. doi:10.1136/bmj.324.7344.1010.

Green, Hardy. 2010. *The Company Town: The Industrial Edens and Satanic Mills That Shaped the American Economy*. New York: Basic Books.

Hadaway, C. Kirk, Penny Long Marler, and Mark Chaves. 1993. "What the Polls Don't Show: A Closer Look at U.S. Church Attendance." *American Sociological Review* 58 (6): 741–52.

Haidt, Jonathan. 2013. *The Righteous Mind: Why Good People Are Divided by Politics and Religion*. New York: Vintage Books.

Hammer, Joseph H., Ryan T. Cragun, Karen Hwang, and Jesse Smith. 2012. "Forms, Frequency, and Correlates of Perceived Anti-Atheist Discrimination." *Secularism and Nonreligion* 1: 43–67.

Harper, Marcel. 2007. "The Stereotyping of Nonreligious People by Religious Students: Contents and Subtypes." *Journal for the Scientific Study of Religion* 46 (4): 539–52.

Harvie, Robin, and Stephanie Meyers. 2010. *The Atheist's Guide to Christmas.* HarperCollins e-books.

Hayes, Bernadette C., and Yvonne Pittelkow. 1993. "Religious Belief, Transmission, and the Family: An Australian Study." *Journal of Marriage and the Family* 55 (3): 755–66.

Heiner, Robert. 1992. "Evangelical Heathens: The Deviant Status of Freethinkers in Southland." *Deviant Behavior: An Interdisciplinary Journal* 13: 1–20.

Hill, Patrick L., Mathias Allemand, and Brent W. Roberts. 2013. "Examining the Pathways between Gratitude and Self-Rated Physical Health across Adulthood." *Personality and Individual Differences* 54 (1): 92–96. doi:10.1016/j.paid.2012.08.011.

Hodgson, Godfrey. 2006. *A Great & Godly Adventure: The Pilgrims & the Myth of the First Thanksgiving.* PublicAffairs.

Hoffmann, John E., and John E. Bartkowski. 2008. "Gender, Religious Tradition and Biblical Literalism." *Social Forces* 86 (3): 1245–72.

Hoge, Dean R., Gregory H. Petrillo, and Ella I. Smith. 1982. "Transmission of Religious and Social Values from Parents to Teenage Children." *Journal of Marriage and the Family* 44 (3): 569–80.

Hook, Jennifer. 2006. "Care in Context: Men's Unpaid Work in 20 Countries, 1965–2003." *American Sociological Review* 71 (August): 639–60.

Howden, Lindsay M., and Julie A. Meyer. 2011. *Age and Sex Composition: 2010*. C2010BR-03. 2010 Census Briefs. Washington, D.C.: United States Census Bureau. http://www.census.gov/prod/cen2010/briefs/c2010br-03.pdf.

Hoxie, Frederick E. 2001. *A Final Promise: The Campaign to Assimilate the Indians, 1880-1920*. Lincoln, Neb: University of Nebraska Press.

Hunsberger, Bruce. 2006. *Atheists: A Groundbreaking Study of America's Nonbelievers*. Amherst, N.Y: Prometheus Books.

Hunsberger, Bruce, Michael Pratt, and S. Mark Pancer. 2001. "Religious Versus Nonreligious Socialization: Does Religious Background Have Implications for Adjustment?" *International Journal for the Psychology of Religion* 11 (2): 105–28.

Iverson, Hans Raun. 2014. "Religion in Denmark." *Denmark.dk*. December 16. http://denmark.dk/en/society/religion/.

Jacoby, Susan. 2005. *Freethinkers: A History of American Secularism*. Holt Paperbacks.

Jenks, R J. 1986. "Perceptions of Two Deviant and Two Nondeviant Groups." *The Journal of Social Psychology* 126 (6): 783–90.

Jensen, Gary, and Ashley Thompson. 2008. "'Out of the Broom Closet': The Social Ecology of American Wicca." *Journal for the Scientific Study of Religion* 47 (4): 753–66.

Johnson, Daniel Carson. 1997. "Formal Education vs. Religious Belief: Soliciting New Evidence with Multinomial Logit Modeling." *Journal for the Scientific Study of Religion* 36: 231–46.

Johnson, Megan K., Wade C. Rowatt, and Jordan LaBouff. 2010. "Priming Christian Religious Concepts Increases Racial Prejudice." *Social Psychological and Personality Science* 1 (2): 119–26. doi:10.1177/1948550609357246.

Jost, John T., Jaime L. Napier, Hulda Thorisdottir, Samuel D. Gosling, Tibor P. Palfai, and Brian Ostafin. 2007. "Are Needs to Manage Uncertainty and Threat Associated With Political Conservatism or Ideological Extremity?" *Pers Soc Psychol Bull* 33 (7): 989–1007. doi:10.1177/0146167207301028.

Justice, Kim. 2011. *Undermining Prosperity: Higher Education Cuts Weaken Access, Affordability, and Quality*. Seattle, WA: Washington State Budget & Policy Center. http://budgetandpolicy.org/reports/undermining-prosperity-higher-education-cuts-weaken-access-affordability-and-quality.

Kaleem, Jaweed. 2012. "Best Paid Pastors Make Hundreds Of Thousands To Millions Of Dollars Annually." *Huffington Post*. January 19. http://www.huffingtonpost.com/2012/01/19/best-paid-pastors_n_1214043.html.

———. 2014. "Presbyterian Church Votes To Allow Gay Marriages." *Huffington Post*. June 19. http://www.huffingtonpost.com/2014/06/19/presbyterian-church-gay-marriage_n_5512756.html.

Kalil, Ariel. 2009. "Joblessness, Family Relations and Children's Development." *Family Matters*, no. 83 (September): 15–22.

Katz, Michael B. 1976. "The Origins of Public Education: A Reassessment." *History of Education Quarterly* 16 (4): 381–407. doi:10.2307/367722.

Kirk, Chris. 2014. "Map: Publicly Funded Schools That Are Allowed to Teach Creationism." *Slate*, January 26. http://www.slate.com/articles/health_and_science/science/2014/01/creationism_in_public_schools_mapped_where_tax_money_supports_alternatives.html.

Kosmin, Barry A., and Ariela Keysar. 2006. *Religion in a Free Market: Religious and Non-Religious Americans*. Paramount Market Publishing, Inc.

Kosmin, Barry A., Ariela Keysar, Ryan T. Cragun, and Juhem Navarro-Rivera. 2009. *American Nones: The Profile of the No Religion Population*. A Report Based on the American Religious Identification Survey 2008. Hartford, CT: Institute for the Study of Secularism in Society and Culture.

Krause, Neal, Deborah Bruce, R. David Hayward, and Cynthia Woolever. 2014. "Gratitude to God, Self-Rated Health, and Depressive Symptoms." *Journal for the Scientific Study of Religion* 53 (2): 341–55. doi:10.1111/jssr.12110.

Krause, Neal, and R. David Hayward. 2014. "Hostility, Religious Involvement, Gratitude, and Self-Rated Health in Late Life." *Research on Aging* 36 (6): 731–52. doi:10.1177/0164027513519113.

Kuo, David. 2007. *Tempting Faith: An Inside Story of Political Seduction*. Reprint edition. New York: Free Press.

Laurin, Kristin, Aaron C. Kay, and David A. Moscovitch. 2008. "On the Belief in God: Towards an Understanding of the Emotional Substrates of Compensatory Control." *Journal of Experimental Social Psychology* 44 (6): 1559–62. doi:10.1016/j.jesp.2008.07.007.

Layton, Deborah. 1999. *Seductive Poison: A Jonestown Survivor's Story of Life and Death in the People's Temple*. New York: Anchor.

LeDrew, Stephen. 2012. "The Evolution of Atheism Scientific and Humanistic Approaches." *History of the Human Sciences* 25 (3): 70–87. doi:10.1177/0952695112441301.

———. 2013. "Discovering Atheism: Heterogeneity in Trajectories to Atheist Identity and Activism." *Sociology of Religion*, 74 (4): 431–453. doi:10.1093/socrel/srt014.

Lee, Jenny J. 2002. "Religion and College Attendance: Change among Students." *The Review of Higher Education* 25 (4): 369–84.

Leopold, Anita Maria, and Jeppe Sinding Jensen, eds. 2004. *Syncretism in Religion: A Reader*. New York: Routledge.

Levack, Brian P. 2006. *The Witch-Hunt in Early Modern Europe*. 3rd edition. Harlow, England ; New York: Routledge.

Lichter, Daniel T., Richard N. Turner, and Sharon Sassler. 2010. "National Estimates of the Rise in Serial Cohabitation." *Social Science Research* 39 (5): 754–65.

Litman, Jordan A., and Charles D. Spielberger. 2003. "Measuring Epistemic Curiosity and Its Diversive and Specific Components." *Journal of Personality Assessment* 80 (1): 75–86. doi:10.1207/S15327752JPA8001_16.

Livingston, Elizabeth A. 2008. "A Bright Line Points Toward Legal Compromise: IRS Condoned Lobbying Activities for Religious Entities and Non-Profits." *Rutgers Journal of Law and Religion* 9 (1): 1–26.

Logel, Christine, Gregory M. Walton, Steven J. Spencer, Emma C. Iserman, William von Hippel, and Amy E. Bell. 2009. "Interacting With Sexist Men Triggers Social Identity Threat Among Female Engineers." *Journal of Personality & Social Psychology* 96 (6): 1089–1103.

Losee, John. 2001. *A Historical Introduction to the Philosophy of Science, 4th Edition*. New York: Oxford University Press.

Lugo, Luis, Alan Cooperman, Cary Funk, and Gregory A. Smith. 2012. *"Nones" on the Rise: One-in-Five Adults Have No Religious Affiliation*. Washington, D.C.: The Pew Forum on Religion & Public Life. http://www.pewforum.org/Unaffiliated/nones-on-the-rise.aspx.

Mansbridge, Jane J. 1986. *Why We Lost the ERA*. Chicago: University Of Chicago Press.

Markovich, Steven J. 2012. "Promoting Innovation Through R&D." *Council on Foreign Relations*. November 5. http://www.cfr.org/innovation/promoting-innovation-through-rd/p29403.

Martin, Bernice. 2006. "Pentecostal Conversion And The Limits Of The Market Metaphor." *Exchange* 35 (1): 61–91. doi:10.1163/157254306776066951.

McCann, Carole R. 1999. *Birth Control, Politics in the United States, 1916-1945*. Ithaca: Cornell University Press.

McKinley Jr., James C. 2010. "Texas Conservatives Win Curriculum Change." *The New York Times*, March 12, sec. Education. http://www.nytimes.com/2010/03/13/education/13texas.html.

Mehta, Hemant. 2013. "Atheist Opens Up About Getting Sexually Assaulted at Conference." *Friendly Atheist*. July 29. http://www.patheos.com/blogs/friendlyatheist/2013/07/29/atheist-opens-up-about-getting-sexually-assaulted-at-conference/.

Merino, Stephen M. 2011. "Irreligious Socialization? The Adult Religious Preferences of Individuals Raised with No Religion." *Secularism and Nonreligion* 1 (0): 1–16.

Michaelson, Jay. 2014. "Iran's New Gay Executions." *The Daily Beast*. August 12. http://www.thedailybeast.com/articles/2014/08/12/iran-s-new-gay-executions.html.

Miller, Alan S, and Rodney Stark. 2002. "Gender and Religiousness: Can Socialization Explanations Be Saved?" *American Journal of Sociology* 107 (6): 1399–1423. doi:10.1086/342557.

Monroe, Bryan. 2010. "How Texas' School Board Tried to Pretend Slavery Never Happened and Why Your Kid's School May Be Next." *Huffington Post*. May 24. http://www.huffingtonpost.com/bryan-monroe/how-texas-school-board-tr_b_586633.html.

Moore, R. Laurence. 1995. *Selling God: American Religion in the Marketplace of Culture*. New York: Oxford University Press.

Moore, Robert A. 1983. "The Impossible Voyage of Noah's Ark." *Creation/Evolution Journal* 4 (1): 1–43.

Morris, Aldon D. 1984. *The Origins of the Civil Rights Movement*. New York: The Free Press.

Murphy, Ryan, Sarah Zemore, and Nina Mulia. 2014. "Housing Instability and Alcohol Problems during the 2007-2009 US Recession: The Moderating Role of Perceived Family Support." *Journal of Urban Health* 91 (1): 17–32. doi:10.1007/s11524-013-9813-z.

Myers, Scott M. 1996. "An Interactive Model of Religiosity Inheritance: The Importance of Family Context." *American Sociological Review* 61 (5): 858–66.

National Geographic Channel. 2008. *Inside a Cult*. National Geographic Channel. http://channel.nationalgeographic.com/channel/episodes/inside-a-cult2/.

National Science Foundation. 2014. "NSF Study Shows Declines in Federal Funding for Research and Development." *National Science Foundation*. January 15. http://www.nsf.gov/news/news_summ.jsp?cntn_id=130156.

newsinenglish.no. 2009. "Church Attendance Hits New Low." *Newsinenglish.no*. September 30. http://www.newsinenglish.no/2009/09/30/church-attendance-hits-new-low/.

Norenzayan, Ara. 2013. *Big Gods How Religion Transformed Cooperation and Conflict*. Princeton: Princeton University Press.

Norris, Pippa, and Ronald Inglehart. 2004. *Sacred and Secular: Religion and Politics Worldwide*. Cambridge University Press.

Nutini, Hugo G. 1976. "Syncretism and Acculturation: The Historical Development of the Cult of the Patron Saint in Tlaxcala, Mexico (1519-1670)." *Ethnology* 15 (3): 301. doi:10.2307/3773137.

O'Hair, Madalyn Murray. 1989. *An Atheist Epic: The Complete Unexpurgated Story of How Bible and Prayers Were Removed from the Public Schools of the United States*. Austin, Tex: American Atheist Press.

Olson, Paul J. 2006. "The Public Perception of 'Cults' and 'New Religious Movements.'" *Journal for the Scientific Study of Religion* 45 (1): 97–106.

Oreskes, Naomi. 2002. *Plate Tectonics: An Insider's History Of The Modern Theory Of The Earth*. 1st edition. Boulder, Colo: Westview Press.

Pasquale, Frank L. 2010. "A Portrait of Secular Group Affiliates." In *Atheism and Secularity: Volume 1 - Issues, Concepts, and Definitions*, edited by Phil Zuckerman, 1:43–88. Santa Barbara, CA: Praeger.

Pérez, Joseph. 2006. *The Spanish Inquisition: A History*. Translated by Janet Lloyd. New Haven, CT: Yale University Press.

Peterson, Gregory R. 2003. "Demarcation and the Scientistic Fallacy." *Zygon®* 38 (4): 751–61. doi:10.1111/j.1467-9744.2003.00536.x.

Pew Research Center. 2013. *Public's Knowledge of Science and Technology*. Washington D.C.: Pew Research Center. http://www.people-press.org/files/legacy-pdf/04-22-13%20Science%20knowledge%20Release.pdf.

Pfeffer, Paula F. 1996. *A. Philip Randolph, Pioneer of the Civil Rights Movement*. Louisiana State Univ Pr.

Pinker, Steven. 2012. *The Better Angels of Our Nature: Why Violence Has Declined*. Reprint edition. Penguin Books.

Plait, Phil. 2013. "Vouching Against Creationism." *Slate*, January 17. http://www.slate.com/blogs/bad_astronomy/2013/01/17/teaching_creationism_school_vouchers_being_used_to_illegally_teach_religion.html.

Popper, Karl. 2002. *Conjectures and Refutations: The Growth of Scientific Knowledge*. 2nd edition. New York: Routledge.

Posner, Richard A. 1994. *Sex and Reason*. Harvard University Press.

Presser, H. B. 1994. "Employment Schedules Among Dual-Earner Spouses and the Division of Household Labor by Gender." *American Sociological Review* 59 (3): 348–64.

ProQuest Statistical Abstract of the U.S. 2015a. *Table 86: Live Births, Deaths, Marriages, and Divorces: 1960 to 2012.*

———. 2015b. *Table 87: Live Births, Birth Rates, and Fertility Rates by Hispanic Origin: 2000 to 2011.*

Pulliam, John D, James J Van Patten, and John D Pulliam. 2013. *The History and Social Foundations of American Education*. Boston: Pearson.

Putnam, Robert D, and David E. Campbell. 2012. *American Grace: How Religion Divides and Unites Us*. New York: Simon & Schuster.

Randolph, William C. 1995. "Dynamic Income, Progressive Taxes, and the Timing of Charitable Contributions." *Journal of Political Economy* 103 (4): 709–38.

Richards, Graham. 2012. *Race, Racism and Psychology: Towards a Reflexive History*. 2 edition. Routledge.

Ridley, Matt. 2012. "Apocalypse Not: Here's Why You Shouldn't Worry About End Times." *Wired Science*. http://www.wired.com/wiredscience/2012/08/ff_apocalypsenot/.

Rosenbaum, Janet Elise. 2009. "Patient Teenagers? A Comparison of the Sexual Behavior of Virginity Pledgers and Matched Nonpledgers." *Pediatrics* 123 (1): e110–20. doi:10.1542/peds.2008-0407.

Rupar, Aaron. 2013. "St. Paul Saints to Again Become St. Paul Aints in Honor of Minnesota Atheists." News. *The Blotter*. July 30. http://blogs.citypages.com/blotter/2013/07/st_paul_saints_to_again_become_st_paul_aints_in_honor_of_minnesota_atheists.php.

Ryan, Christopher, and Cacilda Jethá. 2011. *Sex at Dawn: How We Mate, Why We Stray, and What It Means for Modern Relationships*. New York, NY: Harper.

Sager, Rebecca. 2009. *Faith, Politics, and Power : The Politics of Faith-Based Initiatives: The Politics of Faith-Based Initiatives*. Oxford University Press.

Sandage, Steven J., Peter C. Hill, and Deanne C. Vaubel. 2011. "Generativity, Relational Spirituality, Gratitude, and Mental Health: Relationships and Pathways." *International Journal for the Psychology of Religion* 21 (1): 1–16. doi:10.1080/10508619.2011.532439.

Santelli, John, Mary A. Ott, Maureen Lyon, Jennifer Rogers, Daniel Summers, and Rebecca Schleifer. 2006. "Abstinence and Abstinence-Only Education: A Review of U.S. Policies and Programs." *Journal of Adolescent Health* 38 (1): 72–81. doi:10.1016/j.jadohealth.2005.10.006.

Sappleton, Natalie, and Haifa Takruri-Rizk. 2008. "The Gender Subtext of Science, Engineering, and Technology (SET) Organizations: A Review and Critique." *Women's Studies* 37 (3): 284–316. doi:10.1080/00497870801917242.

Saward, John. 2014. "This American Bro: A Portrait of the Worst Guy Ever." *VICE*. March 21. http://www.vice.com/read/this-american-bro-an-ethological-study.

Scheeres, Julia. 2012. *A Thousand Lives: The Untold Story of Jonestown*. Reprint edition. New York: Free Press.

Schrock, Douglas, and Michael Schwalbe. 2009. "Men, Masculinity, and Manhood Acts." *Annual Review of Sociology* 35 (1): 277–95. doi:10.1146/annurev-soc-070308-115933.

Scott, Jacqueline. 1998. "Changing Attitudes to Sexual Morality: A Cross-National Comparison." *Sociology* 32 (4): 815–45.

Sered, Susan Starr. 1994. "Ideology, Autonomy, and Sisterhood: An Analysis of the Secular Consequences of Women's Religions." *Gender & Society* 8 (4): 486–506.

———. 1998. "'Woman' as Symbol and Women as Agents: Gendered Religious Discourses and Practices." In *Revisioning Gender*, edited by Myra Marx Ferree, Judith Lorber, and Beth B. Hess, 193–221. Thousand Oaks, CA: Sage Publications.

Settles, Isis H., Lilia M. Cortina, Nicole T. Buchanan, and Kathi N. Miner. 2013. "Derogation, Discrimination, and (Dis)Satisfaction With Jobs in Science: A Gendered Analysis." *Psychology of Women Quarterly* 37 (2): 179–91. doi:10.1177/0361684312468727.

Song, Chorong, Dawou Joung, Harumi Ikei, Miho Igarashi, Mariko Aga, Bum-Jin Park, Masayuki Miwa, Michiko Takagaki, and Yoshifumi Miyazaki. 2013. "Physiological and Psychological Effects of Walking on Young Males in Urban Parks in Winter." *Journal of Physiological Anthropology* 32: 18. doi:10.1186/1880-6805-32-18.

Stark, Rodney. 2013. *America's Blessings: How Religion Benefits Everyone, Including Atheists*. Templeton Press.

Stark, Rodney, and Roger Finke. 2000. *Acts of Faith: Explaining the Human Side of Religion*. California: University of California Press.

Stengers, Jean, and Anne Van Neck. 2001. *Masturbation: The History of a Great Terror*. Translated by Kathryn Hoffmann. 1St Edition edition. New York: Palgrave Macmillan Trade.

Stewart, Katherine. 2012. *The Good News Club: The Christian Right's Stealth Assault on America's Children*. New York: PublicAffairs.

Stolzenberg, Ross M., Mary Blair-Loy, and Linda J. Waite. 1995. "Religious Participation in Early Adulthood: Age and Family Life Cycle Effects on Church Membership." *American Sociological Review* 60 (1): 84–103.

Talbot, Steve. 2006. "Spiritual Genocide: The Denial of American Indian Religious Freedom, from Conquest to 1934." *Wicazo Sa Review* 21 (2): 7–39. doi:10.1353/wic.2006.0024.

taxfoundation.org. 2013. "U.S. Federal Individual Income Tax Rates History, 1862-2013 (Nominal and Inflation-Adjusted Brackets)." *Tax Foundation*. October 17. blog.

Taylor, Alan. 2002. *American Colonies: The Settling of North America, Vol. 1*. Reprint edition. New York: Penguin Books.

The Associated Press. 2012. "Obama Hosting Ramadan Dinner At White House." *Huffington Post*. August 10. http://www.huffingtonpost.com/2012/08/10/obama-ramadan-dinner-iftar_n_1763758.html.

The Marx-Engels Reader. 1978. 2d ed. New York: Norton.

Thompson Coon, J., K. Boddy, K. Stein, R. Whear, J. Barton, and M. H. Depledge. 2011. "Does Participating in Physical Activity in Outdoor Natural Environments Have a Greater Effect on Physical and Mental Wellbeing than Physical Activity Indoors? A Systematic Review." *Environmental Science & Technology* 45 (5): 1761–72. doi:10.1021/es102947t.

Thompson, Edward H. Jr., and Kathryn R. Remmes. 2002. "Does Masculinity Thwart Being Religious? An Examination of Older

Men's Religiousness." *Journal for the Scientific Study of Religion.*

Thornton, Arland, William G. Axinn, and Daniel H. Hill. 1992. "Reciprocal Effects of Religiosity, Cohabitation, and Marriage." *American Journal of Sociology* 98 (3): 628–51.

Tice, Dianne M. 1992. "Self-Concept Change and Self-Presentation: The Looking Glass Self Is Also a Magnifying Glass." *Journal of Personality and Social Psychology* 63 (3): 435–51. doi:http://dx.doi.org.esearch.ut.edu/10.1037/0022-3514.63.3.435.

Twain, Mark. 2014. *Captain Stormfield's Visit to Heaven.* CreateSpace Independent Publishing Platform.

United Church of Christ. 1985. "Resolution 'Calling on UCC Congregations to Covenant as Open and Affirming.'" *Ucc.org.* http://www.ucc.org/men/open-and-affirming.html.

———. 2005. "In Support of Equal Marriage Rights for All." http://www.ucc.org/assets/pdfs/in-support-of-equal-marriage-rights-for-all-with-background.pdf.

Urbina, Ian. 2009. "Delaware Diocese Files for Bankruptcy in Wake of Abuse Suits." *The New York Times,* October 20, sec. US. http://www.nytimes.com/2009/10/20/us/20delaware.html.

U.S. Census Bureau. 2012. *Statistical Abstract of the United States.* 131st Edition. Washington, D.C.: U.S. Census Bureau. http://www.census.gov/compendia/statab/.

———. 2013. "Educational Attainment in the United States: 2013." *Census.gov.* http://www.census.gov/hhes/socdemo/education/data/cps/2013/tables.html.

U.S. Census Bureau Public Information Office. 2012. "U.S. Census Bureau Projections Show a Slower Growing, Older, More Diverse Nation a Half Century from Now." *Census.gov.* December 12. https://www.census.gov/newsroom/releases/archives/population/cb12-243.html.

U.S. Department of Education. 2012. "Parent and Family Involvement in Education, from the National Household Education Surveys Program of 2012." *National Center for Education Statistics.* https://nces.ed.gov/pubs2013/2013028/tables/table_08.asp.

U.S. Department of State. 2009. *Denmark.* Report. Washington D.C.: US Department of State. http://www.state.gov/j/drl/rls/irf/2009/127307.htm.

Veblen, Thorsten. 2006. *Conspicuous Consumption.* New York: Penguin Books.

Waal, Frans de. 2014. *The Bonobo and the Atheist: In Search of Humanism Among the Primates.* 1 edition. W. W. Norton & Company.

Walch, Timothy. 2003. *Parish School: American Catholic Parochial Education From Colonial Times to the Present.* Washington, D.C.: National Catholic Education Association.

Walter, Philippe, and Claude Lecouteux. 2014. *Christian Mythology: Revelations of Pagan Origins.* 2nd Edition, New Edition of Christianity: Origins of a Pagan Religion edition. Rochester, Vermont: Inner Traditions.

Watanabe, John M. 1990. "From Saints to Shibboleths: Image, Structure, and Identity in Maya Religious Syncretism." *American Ethnologist* 17 (1): 131–50.

Watson, Rebecca. 2012. "It Stands to Reason, Skeptics Can Be Sexist Too." *Slate*, October 24. http://www.slate.com/articles/double_x/doublex/2012/10/sexism_in_the_skeptic_community_i_spoke_out_then_came_the_rape_threats.html.

Weber, Max. 1946. "Science As Vocation." In *From Max Weber: Essays in Sociology*, translated by H. H. Gerth and C. Wright Mills, 129–56. New York: Oxford University Press. http://www2.pfeiffer.edu/~lridener/DSS/Weber/scivoc.html.

———. 2001. *The Protestant Ethic and the Spirit of Capitalism.* New York: Routledge.

Wichman, Aaron L. 2010. "Uncertainty and Religious Reactivity: Uncertainty Compensation, Repair, and Inoculation." *European Journal of Social Psychology* 40 (1): 35–42.

Williams, Daniel K. 2012. *God's Own Party: The Making of the Christian Right.* Reprint edition. New York: Oxford University Press.

Winston, Kimberly. 2012. "Do Atheists Have a Sexual Harassment Problem?" *Religion News Service.* July 12. http://www.religionnews.com/2012/07/12/do-atheists-have-a-sexual-harassment-problem/.

———. "Atheist Parents Take on Christian 'Good News Club' with 'Better News Club'." *Religion News Service.* January 8. http://www.religionnews.com/2015/01/08/atheist-parents-take-christian-good-news-club-better-news-club/.

Witzel, E. J. Michael. 2013. *The Origins of the World's Mythologies.* New York: Oxford University Press.

Woodhead, Linda. 2008. "Gendering Secularization Theory." *Social Compass* 55 (2): 187–93. doi:10.1177/0037768607089738.

World Values Survey. 2006. "World Values Survey." http://www.worldvaluessurvey.org/.

Zuckerman, Phil. 2006. "Atheism: Contemporary Numbers and Patterns." In *The Cambridge Companion to Atheism*, edited by Michael Martin, 1st ed., 47–68. Cambridge University Press.

———. 2008. *Society without God: What the Least Religious Nations Can Tell Us About Contentment.* NYU Press.

ABOUT THE AUTHOR

Ryan T. Cragun is an associate professor of sociology at the University of Tampa and the author of *Could I Vote for a Mormon for President?* and *What You Don't Know about Religion (but Should)*. His research is regularly featured in national media. He lives in Tampa, Florida.